Praise

I am forever blessed for having read *Call Me Vivian*. I felt the presence of God and his Holy Spirit speaking to me. I pray that God continues to use Katie Scheller to minister to his lost and wounded lambs.

James Earl Quant Jr., inmate, Wyoming

I try to make it a habit to write to an author when he or she has written something that has reached me and attached to my soul. I am so thankful that Jesus, in his awesome orchestrating abilities, allowed Katie's path and my path to converge by placing her book into my hands.

Amy Davidson, inmate, Tennessee

I am touched and inspired by Katie Scheller's journey. The miracles and revelations that transpired in her life could only have come from the great God we serve. May the Lord continue to provide for The Vivian Foundation.

Cynthia Houvenel, inmate, California

I read *Call Me Vivian* and could not believe the similarities between Katie's life and mine. Thank you for the inspiration to never ever give up.

Nicki Bibbs, inmate, Virginia

Katie's story feels so much like my own. I have resolved to use whatever time I have been given here on earth to draw closer to God.

Angela Greer, inmate, Australia

I'm fighting a war every day. I still have a lot of work to do, but thanks to Katie Scheller and *Call Me Vivian*, I understand I'm no longer doing it alone! God's got my back.

Katy Judd, inmate, North Carolina

Call Me Vivian is such an uplifting, inspiring testimony for which I am grateful. This book has touched me and many others here at the institution.

Viviana Rivas-Gunn, inmate, Washington

I have distributed *Call Me Vivian* to our chapel and state libraries, and every unit has several copies as well. This book is not only touching inmates but also staff. Our chaplain has since expressed what a wonderful book it is.

Pamela Smith, inmate and Angel Network Librarian, Washington

Call Me Vivian gave me a hope and a great outlook on life. God gives the toughest battles to his strongest soldiers.

Crystal Morris, inmate, Florida

Call Me Vivian gave me hope when I had none. It's an easy, relatable story and helped me realize I don't have to keep struggling.

Janelle Jesuca, inmate, Florida

Call Me Vivan was like a divine intervention from God. I felt the Holy Spirit speaking to me and could not believe what I was reading; it was like I was reading pieces of my own story. I know now that all things are possible with God.

Giuliana Bosco, inmate, California

I was feeling hopeless when *Call Me Vivian* gave me a second wind.

Sonya Pittman, inmate, Alabama

I loved *Call Me Vivian*. It made me laugh, cry, and grow closer to the Lord.

Daniel Kiss, inmate, Australia

I finished reading *Call Me Vivian*, and Katie Scheller's journey was compelling. Her inspiring message surely transformed some of the women's hearts to trust God for their future.

Faye Boyd, volunteer, Forgiven Ministry, Inc. and One Day with God camp

Katie Scheller presented *Call Me Vivian* and her story at the Milwaukee Correctional Institution for Women. The gospel is weaved into Katie's message, and her story shows that overcoming sin is possible by filling the void in your heart with the one and only true source of love: God.

Diane Rolfs, ministry lead, Eastbrook Church Prison

I've been trying to find the right words to express how much *Call Me Vivian* changed the course of my life. I'm convinced that God spoke to me through Katie's book. It brought me closer to God, gave me hope, restored my faith, and gave me the strength to press on during a very dark season. Since reading her book, I have been on a wonderful journey of recovery. I can't thank Katie enough for her inspiration.

Alisa Johns Snow, former inmate, Oklahoma

Call Me Vivian renewed my hope! God showed me through her story that he is with me and will never leave or forsake me. Katie's book confirmed everything that I believe and everything that God needed me to know about his love for us.

Alan Marie Lopez, inmate, Texas

I was blessed with the opportunity to read *Call Me Vivian*. Katie gave me something to strive for and helped me learn to forgive myself. I would like to thank Katie for her courage, faith, and continued work, not only in spreading God's Word, but also in her dedication to helping inmates and children of incarcerated parents.

Jessica Marie Flanders, inmate, Florida

Call Me Vivian encouraged me and renewed my hope during my incarceration. I pray that God will bless The Vivian Foundation and Katie's ministry work as she continues to bless those in need. Thank you—from the depths of my soul—for all you do to help others.

Selena Ball, former inmate, Texas

Something about Katie Scheller's story has touched my soul. I was blessed to have found her book at a time when I needed it most.

Racheal Parizek, inmate, North Dakota

Call Me Vivian is a powerful, powerful book. Katie beat the odds. Very few people bounce back from what she has been through and where she has been. I would like to thank Katie for her endless devotion to God and for making the world a better place.

Therrold James, inmate, Louisiana

God placed *Call Me Vivian* in my hands. It's a beautiful testimony and an amazing story about being blessed with the Holy Spirit. God is the only way anyone will ever succeed in life, as evidenced by Katie's experience.

Sonya Kennedy, inmate, Washington

Call Me Vivian is inspired by the Holy Spirit of God. Thank you for this wonderful book, which has been a blessing in my life.

Vivian Corujo Rojas, inmate, Texas

I loved Katie's book and story. It was very touching. Her story made me laugh and cry. It also inspired and strengthened me during a time when I really needed it.

Jacqueline Graham, inmate, Texas

Call Me Vivian has greatly affected me, and I am so appreciative of Katie's story. God, indeed, knows what he is doing and how to use his disciples. Thank you to all who made this book possible. God is using it to speak to people and encourage them.

Jennifer Michalka, inmate, Colorado

I would like to thank Katie for sharing her life story in *Call Me Vivian*. She is called and blessed by God to seek and do his will. I can't imagine having been through all that she has. Yet, she took destruction and made it beautiful by humbly walking God's path. It is my treasure and blessing to know of the work that she is doing with The Vivian Foundation.

Marilyn Brasher, ministry volunteer, Florida

Step into Prison

Step Out in Faith

Live a Full, Surrendered Life
with the Holy Spirit

Katie Scheller

BroadStreet
PUBLISHING

BroadStreet Publishing® Group, LLC
Savage, Minnesota, USA
BroadStreetPublishing.com

Step into Prison, Step Out in Faith: Live a Full, Surrendered Life with the Holy Spirit
Copyright © 2024 Katie Scheller

9781424566129 (softcover)
9781424566136 (ebook)

Cover and interior by Garborg Design Works | garborgdesign.com

Printed in China

24 25 26 27 28 5 4 3 2 1

This book is dedicated to Ray Hall, who founded
the Prison Book Project and who passed away in 2022.
Millions upon millions of books have reached
inmates across the United States because of Ray's vision.

Joyce Hall, I know you and your entire team work tirelessly
to continue this labor of love.

Contents

Preface

In 2011, just before my sentencing for having committed two felonies, God clearly told me to write *Call Me Vivian*. That book tells the story of how my extramarital affair led me to defending myself in a civil lawsuit and facing criminal charges that landed me in federal prison. Little did I know at that time that a lot more writing was in my future!

As my second book, *Vivian's Call*, was undergoing editing in late 2021, God pulled me away to Florida for the winter season. I attended a Christian spiritual event in Tampa during the first weekend in December, and I could not deny the heavenly, angelic presence throughout the weekend. The fire of God fell upon me multiple times. At one point, the speaker at the event reminded the audience that it was time to dream again and obtain our rightful inheritance as children of the Most High God. That message struck me, and the following night, I had a dream in which I saw a book in a classroom. When I woke up, I started writing down everything God was telling me. Not long after, he showed me a vision of a book cover, and what you are holding in your hands is the result of that very dream.

What you may not know is that I wrote emails to friends and family every day during the 740 days of my incarceration, detailing events and experiences in both the natural and supernatural worlds. These emails served as a journal, capturing everything the Holy Spirit taught me and the stories I penned in *Call Me Vivian* and *Vivian's Call*. The interesting part, which I was unaware of at the time, was that my daily email correspondence from prison was blessing others.

Step Into Prison, Step Out in Faith

Just like the apostle Paul, my writing became a living and breathing testament of the transforming power of God's love. My prison time came alive with excitement and anticipation of what God was doing not only in my life but also in the lives of others who walked this journey with me. God was blessing and changing hearts both inside and outside prison walls and teaching me invaluable lessons.

It's time I share these lessons and the rest of my story. And trust me when I tell you that there is hope—even when things feel hopeless. Even when you feel like you are alone, God is always with you. He has a plan for each and every one of us, and the Bible promises us this in Jeremiah 29:11: "'I know the plans I have for you,' says the LORD. 'They are plans for good and not for disaster, to give you a future and a hope.'"

God loves you, and there's nothing you have done or could do to lose his love. He wants to meet you right where you are and become an integral part of your life. If you are willing to trust him, surrender to his way of doing things, and let the Holy Spirit guide your steps, the changes that will take place in your heart will transform your life and powerfully impact the lives of those around you.

You have been called. You have been chosen. You have been set apart for such a time as this. Will you dare to be different? Will you use your remaining time here on earth to serve others in love? Will you embrace the perfect plan that God has for your life? It's up to you. I'm living proof that with God, all things are possible. Receive it! Speak it! Believe it!

Prologue

My meeting with the federal government was scheduled for early February 2007. It was time to tell the truth—the whole truth and nothing but the truth.

I arrived at work ahead of schedule to ensure my calendar was still blocked for the day; my boss didn't know where I was going, and I had no idea how long I'd be gone or if I'd even return to my office.

The federal courthouse staff in downtown Milwaukee was awaiting my arrival, as were a few others. The investigative team included an Internal Revenue Service agent, the postal inspector, a United States attorney, and a federal probation and presentencing officer. My attorney, Michael Cohn, accompanied me to the second floor conference room, which was massive and intimidating. We seated ourselves at a long, glossy wooden table, and the government's team sat across from us. My lawyer and I were outnumbered, but that was the least of my worries.

Prior to our meeting, the investigators had asked me to prepare a document summarizing the supplier gifts I had received while working for my previous employer, SC Johnson. We talked at length about the case, including the company's corporate culture and certain individuals. From there we discussed the gifts I received from my former boss and lover, Milt. The team seemed particularly interested in the jewelry he had given me.

By this time, I had a pretty good idea of what had transpired with my previous employer, given the boatloads of discovery my lawyers shared with me that showed the extent of the corruption in this case. The investigation involved racketeering, which is dishonest and fraudulent business practices. Transportation carriers were providing kickbacks to Milt to secure business, and Milt had been lavishing me with gifts purchased with the proceeds from this scheme.

I told the investigative team everything, including a few things they did not know. I confirmed the evidence against me, and after a reasonable amount of time, much shorter than anticipated, the questioning ended. It felt as though the weight of the world had been lifted from my shoulders.

"That went well, Katie, really well!" Michael said confidently as we prepared to leave. He was pleased, and his hopeful demeanor lifted my spirits. Only one question remained: Would the truth *actually* set me free? I would not get an answer for some time, but it did not seem to matter that particular day. I had survived.

Chapter 1

I t was twenty-nine days into 2009, and the month of well-intentioned resolutions and plans for self-improvement had all but slipped through my fingers. I was on my way to a meeting with my attorney, Michael Cohn, and I couldn't help but find it a bit ironic that I parked on the ramp of an athletic club. I typically used the athletic club's parking ramp whenever I met with Michael because of its proximity to his office. And I could park there for free.

I climbed out of my vehicle, and the slam of my car door pulled me out of my thoughts, reminding me of what I was preparing to face. After my meeting with Michael, I was due in federal court to plead guilty to two felonies. My life was in the process of a vast and vital makeover, to say the least. Was I nervous? Yes. Was I scared? A little. Was I ready to get this mess behind me? Absolutely.

I walked through the lobby of the athletic club because of the January cold and found myself in step with a younger African American man on the other side of the window. I had never seen him before. Other than his blue coat, stocking cap, and general existence, I was too absorbed in my own thoughts to take note of his particular features. *Am I wearing the right outfit?* I wondered. *Would my antiperspirant last through the afternoon's proceedings? Would the media be in court? How would I pay my attorney's bill for the extended day at the courthouse?*

Fewer than thirty seconds later, as I stood on the corner waiting for the crosswalk to grant me permission to cross the street, the man I had seen through the window stood next to me. He greeted me with a hello and a plea for help. He said he was looking for a place to get assistance.

Wanting to keep moving to avoid freezing, I stalled to reply. You'll have to believe me when I tell you that, in the Midwest, the winter wind bites like an angry pit bull. The leaders of cities like Milwaukee, which flank the shores of the Great Lakes, should warn visitors that the unforgiving gusts of winter's wrath really do chill a person to the bone.

I was not sure if this young man was homeless, hungry, or planning to steal my purse, but he seemed nice and was certainly polite. More importantly, he needed help, and on that particular day, who was I to judge another human being?

I told him I was not from the immediate area and that I was sorry I could not direct him. He explained how his journey for assistance had led him to a shelter, but the shelter could not help. He had tried the Salvation Army and a number of other places, too, all without any luck.

The man shared his frustration: "I must have talked to one hundred people, and no one can help me." Shaking his head and half laughing, he continued, "I've had to drink so much water over the last two days that I'm starting to feel like a dolphin."

Water is not enough to sustain a person, so I asked him if he was hungry, and he said he was. Before I could say anything more, he resigned to what he believed was yet another rejection. He said he was heading back to the Greyhound bus station, but I stopped him. I told him I would like to help him, but he would have to walk one more block with me until we reached the lobby of my attorney's office.

We continued our trek, and I asked him where he was from. "St. Paul," he said. I casually mentioned that my son lived in Minnesota, not far from St. Paul. We shivered, victims of Wisconsin's frigid temperatures, as we reached the building. When we stepped inside, he told me he was in town for a funeral and that someone had since stolen his suit. *Why would someone steal his suit?* I wondered.

Within the safety of the building, I retrieved two fifty-dollar bills from my purse and handed the money to the gentleman. "I can't buy you a new suit," I said, "but I can help you get home and get something to eat." His eyes stretched to the size of saucers as he stared at the money in the palm of his thawing hand. His expression showed disbelief and gratitude, and he softly thanked me.

"No booze and only healthy food," I stated firmly while pointing my finger at him, as if I had any control over what he chose to do with his newfound wealth.

I gathered my belongings and prepared to walk away from him and toward Michael's office when he asked my name. I told him, and then he approached me with his right hand extended. We shook hands. "God bless you," he said. I was convinced, at that moment, that he was an angel. Warm tears filled my eyes as we parted ways. Here I was facing one of the most difficult days of my life, and God wanted me to know that he was with me.

Exhausted after my day in court, I looked like I had aged ten years over the last week. Dark circles shadowed my eyes, as if I had just gone ten rounds with a championship fighter. In some ways I had. I was beat up, worn out, and humbled beyond words. *How in the world could this be happening?* I thought. Every time I relived the events, I would break down and cry. *Had I done the right thing by pleading guilty?* Through tears, I uttered a barely audible yes.

I was guilty of count eight: misprision of a felony because "I was aware of kickbacks in the Transportation Department at SC Johnson, and I encouraged a coworker to not talk to authorities as they lacked evidence." I was also guilty of count nine: making a false statement. "I made a false statement regarding the company's gift policy. I stated that I had not accepted gifts, when indeed I had accepted gifts in excess of $100."

Judge Clevert's final question made me pause: "So, Ms. Scheller, how is it that you find yourself in this situation?"

This was not the happily-ever-after I had planned. The character I had been playing for the last fifteen years, Vivian, the kept woman from the movie *Pretty Woman*, had finally realized that her former lover, Milt, would never climb her fire escape and present a bouquet of flowers like Edward Lewis did.

Feeling tremendous shame and humiliation, I sat in silence, searching for the right words. After close to a minute, I composed myself and took a deep breath. My voice cracked as I said, "I slept with the boss." I stated my guilt and the reason why. Somehow, though, the punishment did not seem to fit the crime.

Having just pled guilty to two felonies, the judge ordered another drug test. I once again was led into the basement of the federal courthouse to pee in a cup in front of a probation officer. My bodily functions now required a witness. Judge Clevert also limited my travel. If I wanted to go anywhere, then I would have to get the court's permission. I thought to myself, *You have got to be kidding me. I'm not a criminal.* As if it were any comfort, I was right; I wasn't a criminal. That morning I became a convicted felon.

The probation officer led me to the elevator, and as we headed downstairs, a warped familiarity washed over me. I had been in the same area earlier in the morning for my booking. During the booking process, a federal marshal led me past three holding cells containing a total of seven men inside of them. The stench of perspiration and desperation was overpowering.

Half kidding, I said to the US marshal, "I must be in the wrong place." He assured me I was not. "What did those men do?" I asked.

"You don't want to know," he replied.

I was definitely in the wrong place.

The first order of business in the booking process was answering questions about my life. My family, my financial situation, and whom I trusted my belongings with if I were ever put in jail. I laughed and wondered who would want all my worldly possessions: a blowup mattress, a television, and a lawn chair. I had officially hit rock bottom.

Then it was on to the mug shot. The picture showed a person I did not recognize. I had not aged ten years; I aged twenty. It was so bad that I begged the marshal to retake the picture. He graciously agreed and encouraged me to smile, but the second photo did not turn out much better.

Next it was on to the fingerprints. Since my mundane life had yet to include the experience of fingerprinting, I expected it to involve three-by-five index cards and a metal tin of ink, like the ones schoolteachers use to stamp "Good job" on their students' papers. Not so. The fingerprints of this generation are digitally preserved for the ease of tracking people. The process was interesting but not one I would recommend.

I could not believe I had just pled guilty to two felonies. The combined criminal penalties for my charges meant I faced a maximum imprisonment term of eight years and a $500,000 fine. I was also responsible for $400,000 in restitution. Several defendants in this case also took plea deals, and the lone holdout, an owner of one of the trucking companies, was eventually indicted. A former stockbroker had already pled guilty to money laundering charges and received a sentence of three years in prison.

It was obvious that I had endured a battle over the last few days in federal court. My eyes remained swollen, and my lack of sleep churned my nausea. Bananas and Triscuits sustained me. I am not sure if this was better or worse than the McDonald's breakfast burritos that nourished me after I was fired from SC Johnson. The truth is that stress plays funny tricks on a person's body. But Saturday morning arrived, and I was ready for my return flight to Florida, where I was living at the time.

Exhaustion consumed me as I retrieved my weekly unemployment check from my mailbox before stepping over the threshold to my apartment. I could not wait to crawl into bed and get some much-needed sleep. My emotions were fried, and I desperately needed new strength. Thankfully, I do not remember much after my head hit the pillow at eleven o'clock that night.

It seemed like mere minutes, but five hours later, I was jolted from a deep slumber. I found myself sitting on the edge of the mattress, my head cradled in my hands. Cries escaped my throat. "I can't live like this anymore!" I bellowed in a voice I hardly recognized as my own. Over and over again, my plea bounced off the surrounding walls. My emotions had me on the brink of disaster, and my desperation escalated. *God, please help me! I can't do this alone. I cannot live like this anymore.* I felt utterly broken.

With one final appeal, I begged in total surrender, *God, please help me.* Then peace suddenly enveloped me. My heart was finally ready to let him in, and God promised that he would never leave or abandon me (Hebrews 13:5). When I was at my lowest moment, emotionally defeated, hopeless, and scared, God was with me. He knew it was finally time for me to contend with the emptiness in my heart; things needed to change.

It had been a tough week, and only a handful of days had passed since my encounter with that cold, hungry angel. The previous days had left me emotionally spent, and I knew that uninterrupted sleep was what my mind and body desperately needed. But as Monday's moon began to make room for Tuesday's sun, a realization hit me like a ton of bricks.

Filled with total amazement, I circled my sparsely furnished apartment in the mystical predawn hours. I could hardly believe what I had experienced. "He was from St. Paul. From St. Paul," I repeated aloud to no one. "It was Saint Paul who had a role in this. It had nothing to do with the city in Minnesota!" Saint Paul, also known as the apostle Paul, spread the teachings of Jesus, and the Bible contains the letters Paul wrote to early Christians.

Saint Paul sent my angel, and we met on the corner of Broadway and Mason in Milwaukee, Wisconsin. The funeral and missing suit suddenly made sense, for it was Paul who wrote 2 Corinthians 5:17: "This means that anyone who belongs to Christ has become a new person. The old life is gone; a new life has begun!" The angel had stated that he was in town to attend a funeral. It was my funeral— the funeral of my previous life. My old ways, my past sins, were gone. Thank goodness someone stole his suit! My angel symbolized and delivered the message that my new life, my Christ-filled new birth, had begun.

Angels are heavenly messengers created by God (Genesis 2:1). They are spiritual beings who discern good from evil and provide insight and understanding as they help guide and protect us on our earthly journey (2 Samuel 14:17). As God's Word says, "He will order his angels to protect you wherever you go" (Psalm 91:11). Given my experience, Hebrews 13:2 certainly came to life: "Don't forget to show hospitality to strangers, for some who have done this have entertained angels without realizing it!"

Do you remember when my angel told me he had been drinking so much water that he was starting to feel like a dolphin? I bet you didn't know that dolphins symbolize rebirth, did you? What makes this encounter even more extraordinary is that Paul, whom I can truly relate to, was applauded for his perseverance and deep faith. Paul is the author of many of my favorite books in the Bible, and he was the guy who did his best work in prison. As unbelievable as it sounds, an angel had touched me on that cold January day.

Chapter 2

As my legal battle continued and I waited for the courts to hear the many motions and issue a ruling, God continued working in my heart. He closed the door on my career, and from 2009 to 2011, he opened new doors that allowed me to focus my energy elsewhere.

I volunteered in nursing homes, lived with a recently widowed woman for two winters, cared for a disabled young man, spent quality time with my grandchildren, and attended numerous Bible studies. I met new friends and attended Christian events, including weekly church service.

Back in April 2005, and because of the civil lawsuit that accompanied the criminal investigation, I bought a townhome in Tampa to protect my assets. I moved there and made it my primary residence. However, given the $400,000 in restitution I would eventually have to pay, I sold the home in 2008. That left me living at a friend's house, which was under foreclosure, and sleeping on a mattress topper on the floor.

On November 10, 2011, I woke up early for my Bible study in Tampa. We were studying the book of Jonah. Many of us, Christian or not, know the story of Jonah and the whale. God had called Jonah to go to the city of Nineveh and warn its people to turn back from their wicked ways. Not wanting to obey God, Jonah escaped on a ship but was thrown overboard during a storm and then swallowed by a huge fish. He remained in the belly of that fish for three days and nights until he asked God for forgiveness. Jonah eventually went to the city of Nineveh and did as God requested.

The story of Jonah obviously teaches us about Jonah, but in some ways, it teaches us more about God. Through Jonah's experience, God revealed that he pours out his wrath on the wicked, but he also pours out his grace and mercy on those who repent. To *repent* means to feel or express sincere regret or remorse about one's wrongdoing or sin. God wants us to repent and turn away from sin because he wants to give us a second chance.

We all experience mountaintops and valleys throughout our lives. Wherever you find yourself now, God knew that you would be here. It's not a surprise to him. And the Bible confirms this to be true.

> You made all the delicate, inner parts of my body and knit me together in my mother's womb. Thank you for making me so wonderfully complex! Your workmanship is marvelous—how well I know it. You watched me as I was being formed in utter seclusion, as I was woven together in the dark of the womb. You saw me before I was born. Every day of my life was recorded in your book. Every moment was laid out before a single day had passed. (Psalm 139:13–16)

God knew you before you were born. He thought about you and planned for you long ago. He sees you as immeasurably valuable. The Lord did not place you here by chance or accident. He created you in his image to be his forever friend, his child. God's very own character goes into the creation of each and every person, so let's talk about his character.

First, God is omnipotent, meaning he is all powerful and possesses all authority. He is often called "Almighty" in the Bible for this reason (2 Corinthians 6:18; Revelation 1:8). Nothing is too hard for him to accomplish (Genesis 18:14; Jeremiah 32:17, 27; Luke 1:37). In fact, the apostle Paul says that God is able "to accomplish infinitely more than we might ask or think" (Ephesians 3:20). God is infinite and accomplishes anything he wills without any effort on his part.

It's important to note the "anything he wills" piece of that statement because God does not do anything that contradicts his nature. Hebrews 6:18 puts it like this: "God has given both his promise and his oath. These two things are unchangeable because it is impossible for God to lie. Therefore, we who have fled to him for refuge can have great confidence as we hold to the hope that lies before us."

God is also omniscient, meaning he is all knowing. Isaiah 46:10 reads, "Only I can tell you the future before it even happens. Everything I plan will come to pass, for I do whatever I wish." Because God is all knowing, we can trust that he's aware of everything we're going through today and everything we will go through tomorrow. When we meditate on this truth, it becomes easier for us to trust him with the challenges and troubles in our lives.

God is omnipresent. To be omnipresent is to be in all places at all times. God is everywhere. We can never escape his Spirit, his presence. As David, a king of Israel during biblical times, wrote about God, "If I go up to heaven, you are there; if I go down to the grave, you are there. If I ride the wings of the morning, if I dwell by the farthest oceans, even there your hand will guide me, and your strength will support me" (Psalm 139:8–10).

We have only one God, but he consists of three divine beings: the Father, Son, and Holy Spirit, which is why we refer to them as the Holy Trinity or the Godhead. "All are equally omniscient, omnipotent, omnipresent, eternal, and unchanging, but each is unique in function."[1] It sounds complicated, but as Charles Stanley puts it: "The Father creates a plan, Jesus Christ [the Son] implements the plan, and the Holy Spirit administers the plan…We do not have three gods; we have one God in three persons functioning uniquely and perfectly."[2]

God the Father, sent his Son, Jesus Christ, to free us from the law. The law of God is also called the Mosaic law, the Ten

Commandments, or the Old Covenant. The commandments were laws issued by God and said to have been written with his very own finger (Exodus 31:18). Humanity came to learn of these commandments from Moses, who led hundreds of thousands of Hebrew people, called Israelites, out of Egypt, where they had been enslaved for hundreds of years.

God led Moses to the top of Mount Sinai in Egypt before giving him two stone tablets inscribed with the laws (or commandments) to share with the Israelites. God's Ten Commandments speak of integrity, respect, loyalty, purity, honesty, truthfulness, and contentment, and they're really quite simple. I've summarized them below.

1. Love God more than you love anything else.
2. Make God the most important thing in your life.
3. Respect God's name.
4. Rest on every seventh day to honor the Lord.
5. Respect your parents.
6. Don't hurt anyone.
7. Be true to your spouse.
8. Don't take anything that doesn't belong to you.
9. Never tell a lie.
10. Be happy with what you have. Don't be jealous of what others have.

These commandments told God's people what they should and should not do, but the people did not have the necessary spiritual power to obey them. They continued to sin, which is committing an immoral act, a transgression against God's law. A logical question would be, "If God's people couldn't be totally obedient under the Old Covenant, then why was the law given in the first place?" The Bible tells us: "If the law could give us new life, we could be made right with God by obeying it. But the Scriptures declare that we are all prisoners of sin, so we receive God's promise of freedom only by believing in Jesus Christ" (Galatians 3:21–22). In other words, God gave us the law because it showed us our need for salvation. It was for our own good.

Before Jesus and because of our sinful nature, we could not have had eternal life with God. But God sent his Son to earth to die on the cross as a sacrifice for all of humanity, taking away our sins and making us right with God (Romans 4:25). That's why Jesus is called our Savior. He saved us from our sin, and now we can enjoy eternal life in heaven. By dying on the cross, "Christ perfectly fulfilled every requirement of the law."[3] He established a New Covenant, and because of him, there's no excuse for not having the strength and power to obey God's commands.

The source of our strength and power to serve and obey God comes from the third person of the Trinity: the Holy Spirit. The Holy Spirit works to ensure that every person feels a call toward God's saving grace (John 14:26; 16:8; Romans 1:19–20). Jesus promised the Holy Spirit before his death: "When the Father sends the Advocate as my representative—that is, the Holy Spirit—he will teach you everything and will remind you of everything I have told you" (John 14:26). In other words, Jesus promised his disciples that the Holy Spirit would help them remember what Jesus had taught them. That same Holy Spirit is in us and is our teacher. We receive the power of the Holy Spirit when we believe in Jesus, accept him as our Lord and Savior, and invite him into our heart. This is also known as being saved or born again.

The term *born again* refers to a new birth, a spiritual birth. As John, a student and friend of Jesus and the author of five books of the Bible, wrote of those who accepted and believed in Jesus, "They are reborn—not with a physical birth resulting from human passion or plan, but a birth that comes from God" (John 1:13). Or as Jesus himself explained it, "Humans can reproduce only human life, but the Holy Spirit gives birth to spiritual life" (John 3:6).

Think of it this way. When we were born, we became physically alive and a member of our parents' family. Being born of God makes us spiritually alive, and now we belong to God's family, also known as the body of Christ.

Jesus used this concept of a new birth when he explained salvation to a man named Nicodemus. Nicodemus was a powerful religious leader called a Pharisee. One evening, Nicodemus went to speak with Jesus. "'Rabbi,'" [Nicodemus] said, 'we all know that God has sent you to teach us. Your miraculous signs are evidence that God is with you.' Jesus replied, 'I tell you the truth, unless you are born again, you cannot see the Kingdom of God.'" (John 3:1–3)

Becoming born again is a wonderful metaphor for the new life we receive from God when we accept Jesus as our Lord and Savior. And this new birth, this fresh start in life, this second chance, is available to anyone who believes in him. To believe means to put your faith, confidence, and trust in Jesus.

You might wonder how you can accept this gift. The apostle Paul explained it plainly for us: "If you openly declare that Jesus is Lord and believe in your heart that God raised him from the dead, you will be saved. For it is by believing in your heart that you are made right with God, and it is by openly declaring your faith that you are saved" (Romans 10:9–10).

Receiving Jesus into your heart is the beginning of your new life with Christ. But you must continue to follow his teachings by being rooted in, strengthened by, and built up in faith. This faith in Christ changes you from the inside out. You live for Christ by committing your life to him, submitting to his will, learning from his life and teachings, and recognizing the Holy Spirit's power in you.

You do not have to be a Bible scholar to have heard of John 3:16. It's one of the most popular verses in the Bible. You might have even seen it printed on signs at sporting events. Tim Tebow himself wrote this Scripture reference in his eye black while playing a national championship game for the University of Florida football team in 2009, after which 94 million people Googled this famous verse: "God so loved the world that he gave his one and only Son, that whoever believes in him shall not perish but have eternal life" (NIV).[4]

Step Into Prison, Step Out in Faith

This powerful verse reveals God's unconditional love for us, his creation. It teaches us the importance of laying down our lives for our friends. Yes, Jesus is our friend. He died a sacrificial death so that we could be free from the bondage of sin and have everlasting life. He stands ready to forgive us the moment we repent, just like he did with Jonah. This verse gives us hope, peace, and comfort that salvation is available to everyone who places their trust and faith in Jesus.

My Bible study class was winding to a close, and I wrote down my prayer concerns. When it was my turn to pray, I could hardly speak. Through tears I shared that I was preparing to face the most challenging day of my life. On November 23, I would face sentencing in federal court. I asked the women in my Bible study to continue to lift me up in prayer.

As I regained my composure and gathered my belongings, my phone rang. It was a familiar number: my attorney's. I quickly exited the classroom to find privacy while we discussed my upcoming sentencing hearing.

Chapter 3

While I waited for my sentencing hearing at the end of the month, I spent two weeks volunteering at Really Good News Ministry in Land O' Lakes, Florida. Ruth Ann Nylen, a friend from my small group, founded the ministry, which, among other things, produces calendars with Bible reading plans called "Just One Word." These calendars encourage "students of the Word" to spend time in the Bible each day and write down what they hear from God. I was helping to develop the 2012 calendar and was also busy writing a press release for Ruth Ann's book *The Radical Power of God*.

On the ride from Tampa, Ruth Ann called to invite me to lunch. We shared a nice meal, but she sensed I was not myself. When we arrived at the ministry, Ruth Ann asked me what was wrong, and I told her how frustrated I was with life in general. The hearing loomed over me, and I was attempting to end my sinful affair and codependent relationship with Milt, my former boss and codefendant with whom I had been romantically involved for almost twenty years.

I had no idea what the future held for me or what it would look like. I felt like I had no control over my own life, and the uncertainty consumed my thoughts. As Ruth Ann always does, she immediately began praying with me, asking God to remove my stress and frustration. I began to relax.

Over the next few hours, I made progress on our ministry priorities but was still having a hard time concentrating. We talked again and did an impromptu Bible study on being filled with the

Holy Spirit. We discussed the importance of being filled with God's power, especially given my upcoming challenges.

Ruth Ann's book, *The Radical Power of God,* has a chapter entitled "Setting Your Anchor in Christ with God's Power." In it, she describes being baptized in the Holy Spirit, which goes beyond receiving the Holy Spirit when we are born again. There are three points to consider.

1. Jesus did not begin his earthly ministry until after baptism with water and the Holy Spirit.

2. Jesus said we would receive the power before we go out into ministry.

3. Jesus said that anyone who has faith in him would accomplish even greater things than he did.[5]

I understood those points, but then Ruth Ann writes that a spiritual language comes with the power we receive from the Holy Spirit. While we were together, she described to me the moment she was baptized in the Holy Spirit and even went so far as to tell me how to be filled with the Spirit, including a special prayer.

"Well, I tried that a few weeks back, and it didn't work," I said. We talked more about my attempt at the special prayer, and then Ruth Ann asked if I wanted to pray for power from the Holy Spirit.

"Sure, what do I have to lose?" I responded.

We held hands, and she asked whether I wanted her to pray on my behalf.

"Why not?" I commented. "You've been at this a lot longer than I have."

Ruth Ann's prayer went something like this:

Dear heavenly Father, we humbly come to you now with our heart, soul, and body, and we yield them all to you. Your Word says that you give the Holy Spirit to those who ask. We ask you to fill Katie with your Holy Spirit and give her evidence of your filling with a prayer language in another tongue. We thank you, Lord, for this special gift, and we receive it now by faith in the mighty name of Jesus.

Then it was my turn to pray. Through tears I uttered a similar prayer and began to feel God's presence tangibly. I was crying and knew with certainty that God was up to something. We could feel his power in our hands, and I felt like I was hanging on for dear life. I asked to receive evidence of the filling of the Holy Spirit with a prayer language, promising the Lord that I would receive it by faith. We ended our prayers with a resounding "Amen." It was an exhausting but uplifting experience.

So what happened? Absolutely nothing. But my expectation to receive my prayer language kept me focused until I finished my work. Ruth Ann assured me as we parted ways that I would receive my prayer language that same day.

I got into my car and thanked God for an incredible day, having felt his presence a number of times. Because of what I experienced with Ruth Ann, I was confident God had taken me to the next level and that the rest was up to me. I finally felt at peace.

When I arrived home, I needed quiet time with the Lord. The house was empty, and I headed upstairs to my bedroom, which consisted of a mattress topper on the floor and a television. But it didn't matter what furniture was in that space; God was going to do a mighty work in that room.

In the dark and on my knees, I lifted up to the Lord every care and concern in my heart. It took only a short time to feel God's presence, and for the fourth time that day, I was overcome with emotion. I thanked God for his love, confessed every one of my sins, and asked for his forgiveness. I told the Lord I was grateful for all the people he put in my life and asked him to shower each of them with extravagant blessings.

I had been praying on my knees for close to twenty minutes and started to feel a bit unsteady. Again, I cried out for God's help, much like I had done on the day I was born again.

God, I cannot do this alone, I pleaded through tears. *Please take me by my hand and help me.*

I lifted my right hand into the air, and at that very moment, my body arched, and an unrecognizable prayer language escaped my lips. My speech was faster than when I speak in English, and it just poured out of me. Even though I had no idea what I was saying, I knew I had spoken in a heavenly language. I had officially spoken in tongues. My future fellow inmates would call my prayer language my "lody dody," and to this day they still use that phrase whenever we get together or talk.

After speaking in my new language, my tears instantly disappeared. Words could not describe the moment, and the only thing I could do was grab my head and smile. God had taken me to a new level in the Spirit, and I couldn't contain my excitement. I walked around my bedroom, repeating, "That was awesome! That was so cool! Incredible! Thank you, Lord. Unbelievable!" I texted Ruth Ann, sharing the details of my experience and thanking her.

It's surprising how little the average Christian knows about the Spirit of God. Most people can tell you a little bit about the life of Jesus and a pretty good idea of God the Father, but they are not quite sure what to think about the Holy Spirit. I was no exception.

The Holy Spirit is the very presence of God within us, and in John 14:16–17, Jesus promises the Spirit to us: "I will ask the Father, and he will give you another Advocate, who will never leave you. He is the Holy Spirit, who leads into all truth. The world cannot receive him, because it isn't looking for him and doesn't recognize him. But you know him, because he lives with you now and later will be in you."

Fifty days after Jesus' resurrection and ten days after his ascension into heaven, the power of the Holy Spirit poured out on the disciples, giving them the ability to speak in tongues and communicate with God: "Everyone present was filled with the Holy Spirit and began speaking in other languages, as the Holy Spirit gave them this ability" (Acts 2:4). As Christians, we call this day

Pentecost, which means "fifty," and we celebrate it because it marks the beginning of the Christian church.

The Holy Spirit does so much more than give believers the ability to speak in tongues. It also indwells and empowers us. Indwelling and empowering serve different purposes. Thankfully, Robert Heidler's book, *Experiencing the Spirit,* offers great insight into the differences between indwelling and empowering.

The indwelling of the Holy Spirit is automatic, and we receive it when we are saved or born again. It lives within us to give us the character of Christ, and it's designed to mature us and help us grow in the Lord. The empowering of the Holy Spirit, or the baptism of the Holy Spirit, is the ministry by which the Spirit of God "comes upon" us with God's power. And through God's power, we become equipped to effectively serve the Lord by ministering to others and changing their lives.[6]

To put it another way, the Spirit dwells in us to give us victory over sin, making us holy, and the Spirit empowers us with tools for effective ministry. It is God's will for both indwelling and empowering of the Holy Spirit to take place in our lives.[7]

A product of the empowering of the Holy Spirit is our prayer language. Our prayer language is to be private and used for intense communication between our spirit and the Lord. This prayer language will not only instruct us but also help us stand up against the Enemy. As Paul wrote,

> The Holy Spirit helps us in our weakness. For example, we don't know what God wants us to pray for. But the Holy Spirit prays for us with groanings that cannot be expressed in words. And the Father who knows all hearts knows what the Spirit is saying, for the Spirit pleads for us believers in harmony with God's own will. (Romans 8:26–27)

In 1 Corinthians, the apostle Paul thanks God that Paul is able to speak in tongues and expresses his desire for every Christian to receive their prayer language (14:18, 22). He goes on to say that a person who speaks in tongues is strengthened. Then in Ephesians, Paul writes, "Pray in the Spirit at all times and on every occasion. Stay alert and be persistent in your prayers for all believers everywhere" (6:18). He encourages us in these verses to embrace everything God has for us, including our prayer language, which is a tremendous gift from God.

I couldn't believe I'd received my prayer language. I prayed again, but this time in English. Lying on my back on the floor in my room, I could not move. My body seemed frozen in time. Although exhausted, I couldn't stop smiling. Total peace enveloped me.

I asked God to continue to fill me with his power and allow me to feel his presence again. I prayed for close to an hour, and as I whispered my prayers, I asked over and over again to be filled with the fruit of the Spirit, the very essence of God: love, joy, peace, patience, kindness, goodness, faithfulness, gentleness, and self-control. I needed to exhibit these godly qualities in my life. I wanted to be a virtuous woman, and I was determined to become a woman after God's own heart.

It turned out that our heavenly Father had another surprise in store for me. November 11, 2011, would prove to be another special day.

Chapter 4

I woke up on November 11, 2011, still floating on cloud nine after having received my prayer language the night before. I planned to spend the day with a friend who had recently moved to St. Petersburg. I could hardly wait to share with her the awesome gift I'd received from the Lord. I was all smiles, like a little kid on Christmas day.

As I reflected with my friend on what God had done, it dawned on me that God had orchestrated my modest living arrangements perfectly. He knew I needed to be alone and without distraction to take my faith to the next level. Where better to accomplish that work than an empty house offering all the solitude I could possibly need?

I returned home later that evening, hopped in the shower, put on my pajamas before crawling under my comforter, and turned on the television. I remember checking the time—8:40 p.m.—when I decided to turn off the lights and call it a night.

Lying on my mattress topper in the dark, I began to pray. Within five minutes I felt God's presence. It's difficult to explain how it feels when God's Spirit aligns with yours, but my back arched toward the ceiling, and I almost felt like I was floating.

I pleaded with God to remove my lustful thoughts and sexual immorality. If you read my first book, *Call Me Vivian*, then you know I struggled with sexual sin throughout my life. It was driven by loneliness, insecurity, and feeling unloved. The Lord had fixed most of my problems relating to this issue, but I was admittedly not yet freed from the temptation to sin. I wondered if it would ever leave me. Sure, I had enjoyed significant periods of celibacy, but I stumbled from time to time.

I reminded myself that God is patient with our progress and that I should focus on how far I'd come, but I still needed his help. I asked him to rid me of the demons that held me captive my entire life: *Take the guilt, Lord. Take my codependency and take my shame. Please take it all*, I begged. After I shared every prayer I needed answered, I told him I was ready to be transformed.

Between 8:40 p.m. and 11:17 p.m., I prayed repeatedly, asking God to allow me to speak in my prayer language. Eventually, I began speaking in tongues. The inflection of my prayer language shifted from angry and direct to quiet and peaceful. When the intensity of my voice increased, I sensed God's anger directed toward my body as it arched again, shaking and jerking.

The Holy Spirit continued to speak through me. It was inexplicable how prayer was escaping my lips. I was breathing, and yet I wasn't. I remember swallowing and catching my breath for a few seconds, but I couldn't otherwise control my speech or my body's physical reactions. God was casting out my sexual demon just as I'd prayed for him to do.

Thankfully, I did have the capacity to think during this experience. I was not scared because I knew that whatever God was up to was necessary in order to transform me into a new creature in Christ. It was up to me to let God use me as his vessel, so I went with the flow. His purification and cleansing process continued, and the pace and authority of my prayer language demonstrated that God was serious about what he was doing. And it didn't seem easy.

What happened next was wonderful. It felt as if angels surrounded me, holding and guiding my arms. For the next three to five minutes, my arms fluttered in slow motion as if I had wings. An incredible peace came over me, and I stopped speaking. I smiled, convinced I had received wings of my own. It felt nothing short of magical, and I wanted to savor this sensation forever.

The stronghold of sexual addiction was broken—forced from my body. Completely exhausted, I lay still as I was bathed in the Spirit for an extended time. I needed to use the bathroom, but I couldn't quite move yet. Once I could, I rolled off the bed, stumbled downstairs to check the time, and saw that it was 11:17 p.m.

When I climbed back into bed, I asked God for more. I wanted to be back in the Spirit. Flat on my back with my arms wide open, ready to receive God's anointing, I prayed, *God, cleanse me and make me pure.* Within seconds, my spiritual language returned. God was leading me in prayer, but this time it was much more peaceful. My prayers were mostly whispers. Once again, I felt angels carrying me and my arms fluttering. I also sang "Amazing Grace." I cannot be sure how long this second experience lasted; I was too elated to be on such an incredible, transformative ride to worry about the time. The strength of the anointing subsided, and again I was bathed in his Spirit.

I returned to a more conscious state but knew God was not done with me. I prayed simpler, more specific prayers in my natural language: *Clothe me in your righteousness, Lord.* God answered that prayer quickly because I was speaking in tongues again. Peacefully and confidently, I made my next request: *Fill my heart with your desires, Lord. Fill my heart with your love. Fill my heart with whatever hurts yours.* God was using me as his prayer vessel, and I calmly whispered his words, knowing he was in complete control.

By purifying and cleansing me, God made me righteous, which means to be in right standing with him. Some people confuse righteousness with holiness, but righteousness has nothing to do with the way you act or live your life. Holiness is your conduct, but righteousness is who you are, your character, and human effort cannot produce it. It's the nature of God that resides within you, and it's one of the most vital elements of our Christian walk.

You do not come into God's righteousness by "being good." Your faith in Jesus Christ and his redemptive work brings you into right standing with God, and it only comes by the Spirit of Christ working in your heart. It is a love that can only come from God.

The next morning, I woke up feeling like an entirely new person—because I was. Naturally, I was compelled to document the miraculous experience and my reflections on it. I had been writing for hours when my phone rang. It was Milt. I told him that he wouldn't believe what happened the night before and read what I had written. He listened quietly.

After sharing my experience with Milt, he shared that he, too, had a heavenly encounter weeks before mine. Here's Milt's experience as told in his own words.

I am not sure where my thoughts were when I went to bed on Tuesday, October 24, 2011. During the night and somewhere in my deep consciousness, I found myself standing in an unfamiliar, unusual room. I thought it might be a morgue because the room was void of any living person except me.

One wall was covered with drawers of files containing small index cards. The files were named with titles like "Places I Lived," "Jobs I Had," "Birthdays," "The Birth of My Children," and "51 Years of Marriage." Others had darker titles, like "Lies I Told" and "Things I Did in Anger." Then it hit me: the files were a crude catalog of my life! It was an archive of my every moment—the good, the bad, and the ugly.

I started going through the files, much like a small child opening birthday presents. I felt joy revisiting wonderful, sweet memories, and yet others flooded me with shame and regret so intense that I had to close the drawer.

After what seemed like hours, I mustered up the courage to open a new drawer. A cold chill swept through my body when I read the file's title: "Lustful Thoughts." I read one card and was sick to my stomach to learn these moments had been recorded. Anger and fear flooded my mind. No one could ever see these cards. I had to destroy them.

I quickly pulled out another drawer and turned it over, trying to shake out the file and its cards, but it didn't work. I successfully removed a card, but it was as strong as steel when I tried to rip it up. Desperate and crying, I looked at the file name and was surprised to see it titled "People I Shared the Gospel With." I could count on both hands the number of cards inside that file. *This cannot be*, I thought. I had shared the gospel with many people, or at least I thought I had.

Sobs shook my body, and I fell on my knees. No one could know of this room. I would have to lock it up and hide the key. I stood and began to dry my eyes, and then I saw him in the corner of the room. *No*, I thought, *Not him, not Jesus. Anyone but Jesus.* I watched in horror as he opened the files and read the cards. I peeked at Jesus' face and saw sorrow deeper than I could ever imagine.

Finally, Jesus turned and looked at me with pity in his eyes from across the room. I cried again, a deep, hurtful cry, when he walked over and put his arm around me. He did not say a word. He just cried with me. Then, to my surprise, he walked to the files, took out cards one by one, and began signing both our names on each card.

"No! No!" I shouted, pulling the card from Jesus' hand. There his name was, written in a shade of red so rich, so dark, and so alive that I understood it was written in his blood. The name of Jesus covered mine.

Jesus looked at me and smiled ever so gently before taking the card back from my hand. I turned away in shame as he continued to sign every single card. Then I heard the file drawers close. Jesus returned to my side, placed his scarred hand on my shoulder, and said, "It is finished."

Milt's experience blew me away, especially because Jesus uttered these same words, "It is finished," at his crucifixion at Calvary. As it reads in John 19:28–30, "Jesus knew that his mission was now finished, and to fulfill Scripture he said, 'I am thirsty.' A jar of sour wine was sitting there, so they soaked a sponge in it, put it on a hyssop branch, and held it up to his lips. When Jesus had tasted it, he said, 'It is finished!' Then he bowed his head and gave up his spirit." The word *finished* is the same as "paid in full,"[8] and as we discussed in chapter 2, Jesus paid the full penalty for our sins when he died on the cross.

Skeptics might say Milt's experience was just a dream, but even if it was, God speaks to us in our dreams. Joel 2:28 reads, "Your sons and daughters will prophesy. Your old men will dream dreams, and your young men will see visions." The obvious interpretation of Milt's divine experience (or dream) is that Jesus was not only reminding Milt of his salvation but also forgiving Milt of all his sins.

When we sin or do wrong, it's natural to feel guilty. We *should* feel guilty. But we must also remember that shame comes from Satan, the Enemy. Therapists often say that guilt tells us, "I did bad," whereas shame says, "I am bad." No matter what you have done or where you find yourself, if you repent, you are forgiven. No sin is too big for God to forgive. All you have to do is simply believe since "there is no condemnation for those who belong to Christ Jesus" (Romans 8:1).

At nearly the same time, Milt and I had been transformed by the renewing of our minds. Romans 12:2 describes this renewal: "Don't copy the behavior and customs of this world, but let God transform you into a new person by changing the way you think. Then you will learn to know God's will for you, which is good and pleasing and perfect." It took a long time for Milt and me to get to a place where we were ready to accept these supernatural experiences confidently, but the Holy Spirit empowered us to trust his plan. Our stony, stubborn hearts turned into tender, responsive ones.

Both Milt and I had reached the end of ourselves—and the end of our affair—just weeks ahead of our sentencing. And like he did for the disciples, God was preparing Milt and me to enter prison and become his hands and feet inside its very walls.

Chapter 5

With my sentencing date fast approaching, it was time to leave Florida and return to Wisconsin, where my sentencing would take place. Like my dad, I'm always early to things, so I arrived at the airport two hours ahead of my flight's departure to allow plenty of time for check-in and security.

I slowly weaved through the maze of weary passengers in line for security and found myself standing behind a woman carrying a large photograph of a young man with short, dark hair and a closely shaved mustache and beard. I assumed this man was her son. Near the bottom of the picture was an inscription that appeared to be the dates of his birth and death. When she approached the X-ray machine, a TSA agent whispered to a coworker that ashes were being scanned.

My heart ached for this woman, and yet I said nothing. I set my bag on the conveyor, feeling terrible for not showing her compassion or extending sympathy. *How could I be so stupid?* I scolded myself. Thankfully, God is a gentleman and assured me that I would have many more opportunities. I wouldn't miss the next one.

I boarded the plane and settled into seat 12A, a window seat. I could barely keep my eyes open and hoped to fall asleep on the flight. I was exhausted from the week's events: renewing my mind, receiving my prayer language, volunteering at the ministry, attending Bible study, and packing up to return to Wisconsin. I desperately needed to catch up on rest. In just one week, I would be back in federal court.

I closed my eyes, hoping to fall asleep before taxiing from our gate. Minutes later, the passenger in 12B arrived. She accidentally hit my shoulder with her bag and quickly apologized for waking me up.

"Wasn't sleeping," I responded. "No big deal."

The overhead compartment above us was full, so she had to find space near the back of the plane for her carry-on luggage.

Once the plane leveled off, I heard God say, *1 Thessalonians 5:11.* I wondered why he chose to share that verse with my spirit. I hadn't memorized it, and I certainly didn't want to climb over the woman in 12B to retrieve my Bible, which was tucked away in my carry-on bag in the overhead compartment.

"Come on, God. I'm tired," I said quietly.

God repeated it two more times: *1 Thessalonians 5:11.* He was not going to let me sleep until I looked up that verse.

I asked the woman to please excuse me for needing to get something out of the overhead compartment. I pulled my Bible out of my bag, sat back down, and read 1 Thessalonians 5:11: "Encourage each other and build each other up, just as you are already doing." I smiled. God was giving me a do-over.

I turned to the woman and asked, "Do you need to be encouraged?"

The shadows under her eyes and downturned corners of her mouth answered for her, but she said, "Yes. I do."

I wasn't sure if she would open up to me, but I waited quietly. She didn't say anything for a few minutes, but then she turned to me as if she'd finally mustered up the strength and courage to speak.

Her name was Mary Ann, and she was seventy-six years old. Although she appeared physically and emotionally drained, she looked younger than seventy-six. She did open up to me, and what she shared broke my heart. Her husband of more than fifty years had recently left her, her son was serving a twenty-year prison term, and she was estranged from her grandchildren. For the next two hours, we discussed our lives, laughing at similarities and sorrowing over struggles.

The best thing I could do for Mary Ann was ask God for help. We prayed for strength, peace, and patience. We prayed for her son, her husband, and her grandkids. I showered her with compassion and encouraged her with God's love. I also asked God to grant her a good night's sleep.

God sure does direct our steps and arrange our circumstances, doesn't he? He seated Mary Ann and me next to each other. He led me to Scripture, compelling me to reach out to her. He guided my words. He gifted us with special time together. I knew I had made the most of this opportunity, just as he assured me earlier that morning that I would.

Shortly before the plane landed in Milwaukee, Mary Ann asked if I would do her a favor. "Could you please send something encouraging to my son in prison?"

How could I say no? Before we parted ways, she gave me his address at a correctional institution in central Wisconsin, and I promised to send him a Christmas card.

My promise to encourage Mary Ann's son reminded me of something my best friend from high school, Jane, had written about me in her character letter to Judge Clevert. Character letters are written by friends, family, colleagues, and other people who know a defendant well, and the purpose of these letters is to vouch for a defendant's character in hopes of convincing a judge to deliver a lower sentence. It's permitted for defendants like me to read these letters before they're submitted to the court, and I read every word in every letter.

Jane wrote, "Katie wants to move forward in her life, and what would make more sense in this situation is to have her work as an encourager in prisons, where so many women need a word of hope. She would be an inspiration to them."

Was God leading me toward prison ministry? I wondered. I figured he must have mixed me up with someone else.

In the last few days before my sentencing, I started writing a lot. God instructed me to document every detail of my experience. I'd lost weight from the stress I was under, and I wasn't sleeping well either. I was determined to show a brave face to my parents and kids, but on the inside, I was a nervous wreck.

My long-awaited judgment and sentencing day had come. My sister, Susie, and two of my kids, Jenny and Brian, accompanied me to the federal courthouse. We arrived right on schedule and took our seats on the bench outside of Judge Clevert's courtroom. The courthouse itself is beautiful. It was built in 1892 and features heavy Roman arches, marble wainscoting, oak crown molding, stenciled designs, and plaster ceiling moldings. The atrium is open, so you can see people moving about the building's five floors.

Staring up at the floors looming above me, I thought of Daniel from the Bible, specifically when he was thrown into the lion's den. During Daniel's time, King Darius was in command and signed a law that anyone who prayed to someone other than King Darius, divine or human, would be thrown into a den of lions. Upon hearing the law, Daniel went home, got on his knees, and prayed to God. His coworkers reported to King Darius that Daniel was praying to God, and the king then ordered Daniel's arrest and punishment. The king said to Daniel, "May your God, whom you serve so faithfully, rescue you" (Daniel 6:16). And when Daniel was thrown into the den, God sent his angels to shut the lions' mouths so that they would not hurt him.

Another fascinating story of faithfulness in the book of Daniel tells of three Hebrew men: Shadrach, Meshach, and Abednego. When they refused to bow to the image of King Nebuchadnezzar, the king of Babylon at the time, the men were thrown into a fiery furnace. But because of their devotion to God, God intervened and allowed them to emerge from the furnace unharmed (Daniel 3).

Trust me when I tell you that I felt like I was getting ready to be thrown into both a lion's den *and* a fiery furnace. But I remembered a key verse in the book of Daniel is 2:22: "[God] reveals deep and hidden things; he knows what lies in darkness, and light dwells with him" (NIV). I knew that God would rescue and protect me regardless of what happened. Would it surprise you to know that the courtroom to which my case was assigned was numbered 222?

My attorney, Michael Cohn, was already inside the courtroom, listening to how Milt's sentencing played out. The rest of my support team soon arrived, and shortly before eleven that morning, Michael bolted out of the courtroom to report that Judge Clevert hammered Milt, sentencing him to ninety-seven months in prison.

Judge Clevert's reputation preceded him. As one of four federal judges in the Eastern District of Wisconsin, he was by far the toughest and known for siding with the government. So far, though, he had been merciful to the other defendants. One received twenty-eight months, another twenty-four months, a third received sixty days of house arrest, and one even received probation. To be clear, these individuals were involved in the racketeering scheme, but I faced different charges. Still, I was hopeful Judge Clevert would show me compassion and that my sentencing statement would clear up a few things related to the case. Michael was less hopeful and speculated that Judge Clevert had made up his mind long ago.

"We need to change something in your sentencing statement," Michael insisted. I pulled out my statement, noted his recommended changes, and shortened it where I could. I told my kids to expect the worst: prison.

I took my seat at a wooden table near the back of the room, adjusted my microphone, and opened my portfolio. I had been waiting for this day for three years, and as strange as it sounds, I felt relief. I would finally be able to put this behind me and move on with whatever plans God had in store for me next.

While waiting for the sentencing to begin, the US attorney turned around to share a few kind words about the character letters submitted on my behalf. Everyone wrote about my good traits and what a blessing I had been to so many people. In some ways, these letters read like eulogies for my funeral. One comment that I will always treasure came from my friend Kim: "Kate gives with her whole heart because that's the only way she knows." All their words touched me deeply. I hoped and prayed they would help.

"All rise," the bailiff announced as Judge Clevert emerged from his oak-paneled office door and entered the courtroom.

As protocol had it, the US attorney spoke first, then SC Johnson, then my attorney, then finally me. The US attorney stuck to the sentencing guidelines: "Being bright and highly able, Ms. Scheller should have seen this for what it was," he said.

Judge Clevert questioned the US attorney, asking him if the punishment fit the crime. It was as if the judge were pleading with him to say I deserved less time, but the US attorney would not waver. He stood with his hands behind his back and his head held high, and for a rather long period of time, he did not speak. I was convinced God held his tongue.

Up next was a representative from my former employer. Only one problem: the representative was a no-show. That meant it was my attorney's turn. Michael had prepared four pages of notes with excellent arguments and supporting documentation as to why I deserved a downward departure. We had another problem, though; Judge Clevert cut him off before he even finished the first page. He wasn't interested in hearing any arguments as to why I shouldn't spend time in prison. This was not good.

It was my turn to speak, and Judge Clevert let me read my entire sentencing statement. I apologized to my family, to Milt's wife, and to SC Johnson. I tried to clear up the confusion around my job duties, vowing to Judge Clevert that I had absolutely no responsibility for domestic transportation. I reminded him that at no point during the entire investigation were any criminal activities or irregularities uncovered in the area over which I had direct control.

There was some discussion among Michael, the US attorney, and Judge Clevert, who seemed to waver back and forth over the decision. At one point, I thought I was going to receive probation, yet at another point, I thought he was going to lock me up and throw away the key.

Although Judge Clevert believed the genesis of my problem was a matter of my heart, I was still involved in a crime and not truthful when investigators confronted me. "For the most part, the women I see here are victims themselves," he said, adding his perspective that I was manipulated by men. Taking everything into consideration, Judge Clevert felt a sentence below the guidelines was appropriate. I closed my eyes, waiting for him to render his judgment.

"Thirty-six months and one year of supervised release." His tone was firm and direct, and once he declared my sentence, he stood up and left as swiftly as he came.

I took a deep breath. Michael put his arm around me and told me he was sorry. Someone behind me started to cry, but I wasn't ready or able to show much emotion. My sister thought I might be in shock, but it didn't feel that way.

Honestly, I took the news of my sentencing in stride because of my faith. I may not always understand why God does things the way he does, but I know with certainty that he works all things for good. He had told me two years earlier that he would take care of the injustice in my life. The rest was up to me. I chose to trust him, accept my punishment, and be obedient. I had no choice.

Judge Clevert asked if I had any preference on where I wanted to serve my time. The nearest federal facility was in Illinois, but I wanted to request Florida. I needed sunshine, warm weather, and my spiritual support team in Tampa. But when I turned to look at my kids, I saw their tears. I knew they were hurting, and I didn't have the heart to ask for Florida.

Before leaving the courthouse, I texted my friends in Tampa to announce my sentence of three years in prison. Within minutes, I received the following messages from one of them, Paula: *God sees your acceptance and obedience. Expect a miracle! Keep this to yourself. May he get the glory!...Humility, my friend, is to be studied in Scripture...Wow, the Spirit is speakin!*

Still in a good frame of mind as I headed to my parents' house, I called more loved ones to share what happened. Walking into my parents' house proved more challenging. They were waiting, and not much was said. Stress lined their faces, and I hated the position I had put them in. I tried to assure them over and over again that everything would be fine, that this was part of a bigger plan God had for me, but they're parents, and their oldest child was also just sentenced to thirty-six months in prison.

I headed upstairs to change my clothes and realized it was time to do what was best for me. I picked up the phone and called both Michael and my probation officer and told them I wanted to request Coleman, a federal prison just north of Tampa.

In the first week of December, I received an email notifying me that I would indeed serve my time at Coleman and needed to surrender on January 4, 2012, by two o'clock in the afternoon. I cannot begin to describe my happiness. God had answered my prayers.

I spent the next few days researching the Federal Correctional Complex at Coleman. It was a good thing that I'm a creature of habit who loves structure because I was going to get a lot of it. My surrender date was less than a month away, so I booked a return flight to Tampa. Everything was falling into place—just as God planned.

Chapter 6

Back in Tampa, I picked up my car and stayed for a few days before returning to Wisconsin to start checking things off my to-do list ahead of my surrender date in January. My first task was to fulfill my promise to Mary Ann and send an encouraging Christmas card to her imprisoned son. Check. Task completed. I was surprised, though, when I received the following letter in the mail, dated December 14, 2011.

Katie,

Wow. God really does work in our lives at all times. Mail call is the highlight of each and every day. The staff puts up a list of names at 3:30 p.m., and if your name has a check next to it, then you are one of the men who will have a smile on his face because you're getting a letter from family or friends. It had been four days since my name was checked.

The staff put up the mail list at 3:30 p.m. Again, no check by my name. At 7:00 p.m. that evening, they called me to the officer's station. I got up there, and a staff member handed me an envelope. He said it got stuck in the mail bag. It was a greeting card from someone in Racine, but I didn't know anyone from Racine. I had to look at the name on the envelope again. Yep, it was for me.

I got back to my room and opened the card. I read "airplane," "Tampa," and "your mother" and knew exactly who you were. I just smiled and shook my head. Here I was having a crummy couple of days, and then I receive a Christmas card from a woman who met my mother on an airplane, listened to my mom talk about our painful times, and prayed with her.

I called my mom the day after your guys' flight landed in Milwaukee. The phone calls I make are timed at twenty minutes, and my mom talked about meeting you for nineteen minutes and thirty seconds. Her spirits were high, and she sounded great. So thank you for taking the time to talk and pray with her on that flight, and thank you for sharing Scripture with her.

Now I want to thank you for taking the time to write me. Since my arrest in March of 2007, I have been on an emotional roller coaster. I have been angry with God, wondering how or why he would want me to hurt so badly. I go to chapel weekly and have come a long way since 2007, when I was very, very depressed. I snuck pills into the jail and took more than seventy-five of them one night. I slept for three days and woke up handcuffed to a hospital bed.

By talking to our chaplain and other Christians here, I believe I have found my sticking point. I believe my ex-wife, family, and even God have forgiven me because I asked, but I can't forgive myself. My two children do not have a father to love and care for them. I can't get past that. I pray on it, and some days I feel as though I have taken ten steps forward. Then I see a TV commercial of a father and his son, and I'm back to square one.

Sorry if I went on here, don't want to dump all my problems on you. I wanted to say thank you and get this in the mail. So thank you, Katie. I hope you didn't mind me writing you back.

God bless and thank you,
Daniel

My heart hurt as I read Daniel's letter. So many kids like Daniel's become innocent victims of their parents' crimes. Many are so young when they lose their parent to the criminal justice system that they never know their mom or dad. Many of their children will be forced to grow up in broken homes while other kids will become all too familiar with social services. God knows how much these realities hurt my heart, and I believe they hurt his heart too.

God understands that we struggle with unforgiveness, particularly with forgiving ourselves, which may be why he prompted me to share with Daniel my personal experience with forgiveness and what it taught me. I learned that if we lived in a perfect world, no one would need to forgive anyone. But we don't live in a perfect world.

Despite our best efforts, we hurt the people we love. Hurt people hurt others and will continue to do so until they learn to forgive. That's why forgiveness is so important. Without it, we live with regret, anger, pain, and bitterness. And carrying unforgiveness in our hearts prevents us from experiencing true peace.

Ultimately, forgiveness is a gift you give yourself. It's filled with love, and it's one of the most precious gifts you can give or receive. Burdens lift, and grudges vanish. Forgiveness restores your emotional and psychological wellness. It is also a choice, and once you realize that you can choose to forgive, your heart begins to heal. Your spirit lifts, and life takes on incredible new meaning.

I printed out my story of forgiveness, addressed another envelope to Daniel, and returned to my mailbox once again. I believed the tangible examples of the Holy Spirit at work in my life would serve as a springboard and turning point in Daniel's.

I rang in the New Year in Tampa, and then I received a second letter from Daniel. He shared some of the challenges of being incarcerated, which were tough to read because they confirmed how difficult it would be not to see my family, especially my children and grandchildren.

But Daniel's letter was also powerfully encouraging. He thanked me for sharing my personal story with him and said it touched many more lives than his own: "Bet you never imagined your story would make it into a prison Christmas service, now did you?"

I paused and shook my head. *No, Daniel,* I thought. *I can't say I ever imagined that.*

Holding on to Daniel's letter, I reflected on everything he had written. His update had come at the perfect time. What's important to note is that I hadn't told Daniel or his mother why I had flown to Milwaukee that fateful day. They had no idea about my plea agreement or sentencing, yet God used our meeting to prepare me for the challenges I would soon face. I was days away from following God into a federal prison, and Daniel's words of encouragement gave me the boost of confidence I needed to believe that my ministry calling and time in prison were all part of God's perfect plan for my life. And one thing was certain: my time in prison was going to be the toughest, most heart-wrenching assignment I would ever endure.

My newfound confidence did not, however, make saying goodbye to my family any easier. The next time I would see them would most likely be in August of 2014, assuming I earned good time credits. My mom and dad were in their late seventies, so my ongoing prayer was that they would live long enough to see all the good that would come from this.

Although I knew my kids and grandkids would be fine, I hated to think about everything I was going to miss in their lives. Three years seemed like an eternity, but that's exactly where I had to place my focus. I was going to stand on the promises made by Jesus: "Everyone who has given up houses or brothers or sisters or father or mother or children or property, for my sake, will receive a hundred times as much in return and will inherit eternal life" (Matthew 19:29).

While I knew the Lord was working everything out for good for me, of course I had days when that was hard to believe. This was especially true on Wednesday, January 4, 2012—my surrender date. My friends, Kim and Diana, drove me to Coleman (true friends drive you to prison!), and it was a relatively quiet ride. I called family and friends, assuring them I was in good spirits, but I was also nervous. We arrived at Coleman twenty-five minutes ahead of my scheduled check-in time, so I spent those extra minutes in the parking lot making the last of my phone calls, noting to them that Coleman didn't look like a prison.

We waited, and a van pulled up. Two correctional officers climbed out and escorted two young women out of the vehicle. The women wore white jumpsuits and were restrained with shackles around their wrists and ankles. It was starting to look more like a prison.

Within a few minutes, a federal officer motioned us to exit the vehicle and asked if I was ready.

"Do I have to come in now?" I asked through the window.

"That would be nice," she said.

I took a deep breath and turned to Kim and Diana. "Guys, it's time," I said. "I have to go."

I opened the front passenger door, grabbed my Bible, hugged my friends, and walked up the sidewalk to receiving and discharge. This was it. No turning back. I waved goodbye, kissed my fingers, pointed to the sky, and silently prayed, *God, this is in your hands. I know you never make a mistake, but please protect me.*

I crossed the doorway's threshold, and my next assignment had officially begun. I was asked to take a seat next to the two women from the parking lot, who were now seated behind a table. I filled out more paperwork, and the staff collected more fingerprints and DNA samples from me. They took my picture for my identification card and performed the dreaded strip search.

For lunch, they brought us hamburgers and fries. The three of us agreed the food was edible. We changed into prison clothes: a brown, short-sleeve T-shirt, elastic, khaki-colored waist pants, and blue slip-on tennis shoes. Then we were taken to the medical center for screenings.

After my physical, it was time to meet my counselor. For the first time, I felt scared. This woman looked like football legend "Mean Joe Greene" but meaner. I was certain she could kill me with one hand, so I answered her questions politely. She told me I was assigned to F4, her unit, and I bunked in 401.

I picked up a large plastic bag containing my bedding, a towel, and a nightshirt and was told to be at the laundry at six the next morning to pick up my uniform. The three of us were assigned to F4, and as we headed to our unit, we watched heads turn, scoping us out.

At Coleman, prisoners are housed in units in four buildings: F1, F2, F3, and F4. Each unit holds about one hundred fifty beds, and between each unit is a large lobby containing four phones. It's also where mail is passed out to inmates. The building itself reminds me of a warehouse with twenty-foot-high ceilings, exposed duct work, red plumbing pipes, and fluorescent lighting.

The cells in which inmates are housed are small, measuring approximately eight by ten feet with five-foot-high cement block walls. Each cell has one set of bunk beds, a small bed close in size to a twin, and three lockers. With three women assigned to each cell, there was barely enough room to turn around.

I was escorted to cell 401, which was next to the bathroom and had a window with a view of a wooded area. I wondered how I was going to sleep on what was basically a metal tray with a thin mattress affectionately nicknamed "The Slab." Thank God I had plenty of practice sleeping on the floor.

I also met my two roommates, April and Tabitha. Both were serving time for drug charges, and both knew the ropes. They helped me settle in, which I was grateful for since the expression on my face must have been a "deer in the headlights" look.

Tabitha had been in prison on three different occasions. The first time she was sentenced to three years, the second time to five years, and was currently serving an eleven-year sentence, having been in federal prison for the last eight years. Repeat offenders are the norm, and many women have incarcerated family members as well.

Seventy-five percent of the women at Coleman were serving time for drug charges. Given the mandatory minimum sentencing guidelines, I met women who were serving ten-, twenty-, and thirty-year sentences. Many were institutionalized; prison was all they knew, which made for major challenges whenever they were encouraged to leave their comfort zone. While agonizing over these realities, I wondered how these women survived.

Over time, I would come to notice that only a handful of inmates serving lengthy sentences ever smiled. Most were angry and bitter. And even though many women had worked their way to camp status after serving longer portions of their sentences in higher security facilities, the wear and tear on them physically, mentally, and emotionally was obvious. Their shoulders slumped, and they moved slowly.

As humbling as prison was, I made a deliberate choice to make every day a good day. Women asked me why I smiled so much and how I could possibly have fun in prison. The truth is that it was easy because I was serving the Lord. He never makes a mistake, and I knew with certainty that this was part of my divine destiny. I tried to emulate this lesson from Hebrews: "You suffered along with those who were thrown into jail, and when all you owned was taken from you, you accepted it with joy. You knew there were better things waiting for you that will last forever" (10:34).

God wants us to be happy regardless of our circumstances. He wants us to enjoy a sense of satisfaction and delight in knowing that he is in control and has a plan for each and every one of our lives.

Trusting that God was in control made life easier. I also made it a point to adopt an attitude of gratitude. I practiced my gratitude one day by writing a list of ten things I was thankful for: "I am grateful for the ability to feel God's presence, for my family and friends, especially my children and grandchildren, along with the fact that God has given me a tender, compassionate heart. I am thankful for the ability to smile, which can lift the spirits of the women here at Coleman. I have been blessed with a positive attitude; I'm learning to be more patient. I find something to laugh about every day, and I appreciate how God directs my steps so that

I can lift heavy hearts with kind, encouraging words. I thank God for surrounding me with angels."

When I left my cell for dinner on that same night when I wrote my list, I saw the most beautiful white dove perched on a porch railing right outside the door. The dove flew down, accompanying me all the way to the cafeteria as I prayed in the Spirit. I stopped and crouched down, and the dove walked right up to me. I could not help but think of this Bible verse: "The Holy Spirit [descended] on him like a dove" (Mark 1:10). What a great reminder that the Lord is with us no matter where we find ourselves.

I knew the Lord was also with me when I met a woman close to my age who surrendered two days after I did. We said hello, and I learned her name was Carol. We hit it off, walking and talking every day. She was a lawyer, and she told me she had prayed that God would send her at least one friend who understood her, given her Christian faith. That friend would be me. We joked that maybe instead of writing a book, I should write a sitcom. Throw a corporate executive and an attorney into prison with a bunch of career criminals, and the sitcom could write itself.

Carol and I soon decided to start a Friday night Bible study. We recruited a diverse group of women to join us, and we held class on the bleachers next to the softball diamond. But we faced a challenge. Nearly 70 percent of the women at Coleman did not graduate from high school, and many did not speak English. The two of us had absolutely no street smarts and did not speak Spanish, so we had our work cut out for us. It made us feel like modern-day disciples. To better understand why, let me first share the story of the first disciples.

One day as Jesus was walking along the shore of the Sea of Galilee, he saw two brothers—Simon, also called Peter, and Andrew—throwing a net into the water, for they fished for a living. Jesus called out to them, "Come, follow me, and I will show you how to fish for people!" And they left their nets at once and followed him. A little farther up the shore he saw two other brothers, James and John, sitting in a boat with their father, Zebedee, repairing their nets. And he called them to come, too. They immediately followed him, leaving the boat and their father behind. (Matthew 4:18–22)

These men already knew Jesus, as he had been teaching in the area and spoke to them. He was now calling them away from their productive trade as fishermen to be productive men of faith instead. They knew what kind of man Jesus was, so it was an easy decision for them to follow him.

When we first started hosting our Bible study, Carol received a download from heaven via the Holy Spirit. She typed up the message using a computer in the library and made copies for everyone in our group. It read,

I don't think it is an accident that this small group is made up of ordinary Christians thirsting for more of the wisdom of the Holy Spirit so that our lives will be pleasing to God and totally honorable to him…I don't think it is an accident that the Holy Spirit has called us together to pray that the fire of God rain down on this encampment and…breathe life into the chained-up souls who long for freedom…

You cannot have love, peace, joy, and a sound mind without the Holy Spirit's active participation in your life. Talk all you want about the truth of the Bible, but the spiritual reality of these truths comes not through human reason but is birthed only by a person wholly yielded to Christ…If you want to travel the storms of the world with the power from above, then the peace of the Holy Spirit comes as a breath, a wind, a chime in the night…at the time and place and to the degree to which you have yielded your life to him who holds all things together: Jesus, the Messiah. Let it be in all our lives.

The first part of Carol's message touched on a critical truth. God does not demand special talents or formal education to serve him; rather, he handpicks ordinary, often flawed people to make a difference in this world. The Bible has story after story of people who made massive mistakes but were later trusted with ensuring the greater good of God's kingdom. David committed adultery. Moses murdered an Egyptian. Saul, who later became Paul, killed Christians, including those closest to Jesus. Peter denied even knowing Jesus, and Rahab was a prostitute. Jonah ran from God, and Matthew was despised. God uses our failures, hardships, and trials for his glory.

Carol's message also captured the utmost importance of surrendering to Christ so that he can become the center of our lives. Like the disciples, we need the Holy Spirit if we want to become powerful witnesses of Jesus' love and then share that love with the people around us. When we do, their nets, like the fishermen's, will overflow. Wherever we find ourselves—be it a prison cell or a board room—our goal is to lead satisfying lives that are living testaments to God's glory, leadership, grace, and goodness.

The other good news is that once we are ready, willing, and able to surrender to God's authority and start a new life in Christ, there is no turning back. This new life may place us in tricky, challenging, and even painful situations, uprooting us from our family, pushing away our friends, and causing us to lose opportunities. But God does us an enormous favor when we choose his path for our life. We might not know where that path will lead us or what twists and turns await us on our journey, but when God wants us to break from our past, he puts people, places, and things into our lives to make the hard times more bearable, more enjoyable. My friendship with Carol, for one, is a perfect example, not to mention the many other women whom God put on my path on this journey. They all mentored, guided, and supported me.

Still, we have to learn to cope with change. If we put our faith in God through all of it, we come to see that he truly does work all things for good. New doors open, new friends appear, and for a while we may even feel on top of the world despite whatever uncomfortable, stressful circumstances we find ourselves in.

I was beginning to embrace the fact that only God knows what we must experience, both good and bad, to change our heart. My positive attitude was a blessing, given where I found myself. But I would never give up because God put me inside those walls to be his hands and feet. The rest was up to me to stay focused on him and the calling he placed on my life.

Chapter 7

Six weeks into my incarceration, God challenged me to write down everything I had learned during my first forty-five days at Coleman. After all, he had told me when I entered prison that, while there, I would embark on a course in "human science," and he was not kidding. So far, my studies had taught me the following:

- Some people are just plain mean, and birds of a feather flock together.

- Bullies are extremely fearful, and their ability to control and manipulate others is determined by the amount of time they have been in prison. They also leverage their size.

- The smallest, most insignificant thing can set someone off.

- Crabbiness is contagious.

- Most inmates use food to cope, and most prisoners wear their emotions on their sleeves. Others sleep their time away.

- Many women feel forgotten and insignificant, and some people just aren't happy unless they are complaining. Many crave attention and get it by being extremely loud.

- There is a sense of entitlement and a general lack of respect among the women. The longer people have been incarcerated, the more possessive they become with their stuff and space.

- There is strength in numbers, which is sometimes good and sometimes bad.
- I see at least one person cry every day.
- Many of the women have kind hearts and are pleasant to be around.
- You can always learn something from someone, and random acts of kindness are reciprocated.
- A simple smile and a kind word can make someone's day; a compliment will make their week.
- Being in prison allows you time to be introspective and teaches you to never take anything for granted. You must work hard to remain positive.
- The Bible says patience is a virtue for a reason.
- Talking about family and friends usually brings a smile to most faces, but not everyone has a family or a friend to talk about.
- Prison will change you, but it's up to you whether it will be a good change.

I reflected on what I had written, and my compassion began to grow. I wondered how God was going to make use of me over the next three years. Could I really make a difference in the lives of these women? Sure, I was up for the challenge, but the environment left much to be desired, and my heart still needed plenty of work.

The day I penned my report on human science, God spoke four words to me: *trust me for everything*. The devotional I received in the mail from a friend at virtually the same time confirmed the importance of trusting him. The takeaway message from the devotion I read that day was to thank God when we're required to be still and to search for him in these times instead of wishing them away:

"Although you feel cut off from the activity of the world, your quiet trust makes a powerful statement in the spiritual realms."[9]

After I finished reading this devotion, God challenged me to list the ways in which he had prepared me for my assignment. The first preparation that came to mind brought me back to my childhood. As a kid, I had fun going away to Girl Scout camp, so I had already experienced and learned to cope with homesickness. And because I attended both a Catholic grade school and high school, I was accustomed to wearing a uniform like I had to in prison. God had also made me a small person, so I fit on my sleeping slab just fine. I came up with more than twenty other examples of how God prepared me for my time and assignment at Coleman.

My new list gave me confidence. I was starting to embrace my assignment when God challenged me again to write down the things he had not prepared me for. Well, guess what? I could not come up with anything, which shouldn't have surprised me considering 2 Corinthians 5:5 reads, "God himself has prepared us for this, and as a guarantee he has given us his Holy Spirit."

Look back on your life and see how God prepared you for the challenges and trials you've experienced. He uses tough, uncomfortable, painful situations to mold and conform us to his image so that we can be his ambassadors to others. The following verses from 1 Peter confirm this: "Don't be surprised at the fiery trials you are going through, as if something strange were happening to you. Instead, be very glad—for these trials make you partners with Christ in his suffering" (4:12–13).

First Peter 4:19 is another verse that encourages us to trust God during hard times: "If you are suffering in a manner that pleases God, keep on doing what is right, and trust your lives to the God who created you, for he will never fail you." The apostle Paul, whom we learned about in an earlier chapter, is a perfect example of remaining faithful to God during tough times: "I am in chains now, still preaching this message as God's ambassador. So pray that I will keep on speaking boldly for him, as I should" (Ephesians 6:20).

Step Into Prison, Step Out in Faith

What is prayer? It's simply talking with God—about anything and everything. He cares about every little detail of our lives. James 5:13–15 reminds us of the power of prayer: "Are any of you suffering hardships? You should pray. Are any of you happy? You should sing praises. Are any of you sick? You should call for the elders of the church to come and pray over you, anointing you with oil in the name of the Lord. Such a prayer offered in faith will heal the sick, and the Lord will make you well. And if you have committed any sins, you will be forgiven." This particular passage centers on healing, but we can pray to God for help with temptation, anxiety, transformation, protection, strength, and any challenge we face.

God answers prayers in one of three ways. He says yes and gives you what you want, says no and gives you something better, or says wait and gives you the best. However, Scripture tells us that we must first be in right standing with him, as "he hears the prayers of the righteous" (Proverbs 15:29). Or as 1 Peter 3:12 reads, "The eyes of the LORD watch over those who do right, and his ears are open to their prayers. But the LORD turns his face against those who do evil." To be in right standing with God, or to be righteous, simply means we have invited Jesus into our hearts, acknowledged his sacrifice as the payment for our sins, and accepted his forgiveness.

Too often, we turn to prayer as a last resort when we're already at the end of our rope. What we want to remember is to make prayer our first response whenever we face a problem. Prayer is and always will be far more powerful than any of our own efforts. All we need to do is pray and watch God's hand work in our lives.

On the same day I received the devotional in the mail and recorded the ways in which God prepared me, I also received a card from my friend Eileen. Her card featured verses from a story in the Bible called the parable of the lost sheep: "If a man has a hundred sheep and one of them gets lost, what will he do? Won't he leave the ninety-nine others in the wilderness and go to search for the one that is lost until he finds it?…In the same way, there is more joy in heaven over one lost sinner who repents and returns to God than over ninety-nine others who are righteous and haven't strayed away" (Luke 15:4, 7).

The first thing to understand with this passage is that the Bible often identifies God's people as the Lord's flock. In biblical times, one hundred sheep was an average size flock for a shepherd of modest means, so each sheep was of great value. It was worthwhile for a shepherd to search diligently for the lost one. This parable, or short story as told by Jesus in the Bible, demonstrates God's love for us. It is so great that he seeks out each and every one of us and rejoices when we are found.

Our job as disciples, or people who believe in and follow Jesus, is to find the lost sheep and bring them back into the fold. Trust me when I tell you that I didn't have to look too far to find lost sheep inside Coleman.

While sharing my spiritual experiences and lessons with friends during a visit, one of them said, "Kate, if anybody can pull this off, you can!" That was the ultimate compliment, and it got me thinking just how lucky I was to have been chosen by God to minister to the lost lambs at Coleman.

Sure, my circumstances behind bars were humble and less than ideal, to say the least—small cells, shared toilets, and meals that sometimes left me ill. But none of it discouraged me because the Lord had reminded me on my sentencing day that humility is to be studied in Scripture.

Humility is simply accepting the circumstances of life according to God's will, waiting on his perfect timing, and trusting that he chooses certain events to unfold—all for his good purposes. But the question remains: How do we humble ourselves, regardless of where we are in life?

One of the ways we demonstrate humility and humble ourselves is through obedience to God. That's why truly humble people only compare themselves to Christ, not to other people. Humble people recognize their sinfulness and limitations, understanding that God has equipped them with special gifts, talents, and abilities to be used to serve others. In other words, they're willing to submit for the good of the team.

Because the Lord had instructed me to study humility, I asked him to put me wherever he needed me—for the good of the team. Once again, as I have learned many times throughout my life, be careful what you ask for because you just might get it. And it turned out that God needed me in the last place on earth I ever thought I would find myself: the kitchen.

My new position as a line server had officially begun, and my starting wage was twelve cents an hour. The daily duties included setting up the food line, dishing out the food, and cleaning the serving area. The neat thing about this position was that it allowed me to interact with virtually every inmate at Coleman.

The kitchen employees represented a wide variety of demographics. Black, white, Hispanic, educated, uneducated, young, and old. The youngest employee was twenty-three, and the oldest, whose job was silverware roller (no pun intended), was seventy-four. When we stood to be counted at four in the afternoon, we really did resemble the Bad News Bears, the team of little league baseball misfits from the sports comedy film of the same name.

Most of the kitchen employees came from broken homes and suffered physical, emotional, and verbal abuse that left them feeling worthless, uncared for, and unloved. I was determined to help bring these ladies to the next spiritual level, which meant it was time for me to step up as a mentor.

My main objectives were to teach them how to believe not only in themselves but also in the promise that God has a special plan and purpose for their lives. Let's just say I had my work cut out for me. My strategy was to meet them wherever they were in their faith journey. Then I could tend to their specific needs as individuals. I knew it would not be an easy job because I first had to build trust with them. That takes time, but I had plenty of it and was in it for the long haul.

On Wednesday, February 29, 2012, just two months into my sentence, a woman I had never met came through the serving line and asked me for the name of my book. I hadn't even told anyone that I was writing a book, so my first thought was, *Who is this woman, and why is she asking me this question?* Nevertheless, I sensed in my spirit that God was up to something and shared the book's title with her.

The next day, while I was serving dessert, the same woman approached me and confidently stated, "It's going to be a bestseller!"

With a smile, I asked her, "Have you been talking to God?"

She returned a smile and said, "Yes, I have."

I was so happy that it felt as if my feet hovered above the ground.

Later, I returned to my unit after lunch to shower. "It's going to be a bestseller!" I shouted as the hot water bounced off my head. I am convinced that the joy I felt in that moment was the exact same joy that David experienced when he danced naked in front of the Lord. I prayed in the Spirit and danced around for thirty minutes, thanking God for what he would do with *Call Me Vivian*.

On Friday, two days after our initial meeting, I saw my new friend again and asked, "Any messages today?"

"No," she said. "Nothing today."

Despite her earlier prophetic message from God about my book's future, I still did not know her name. "Who are you?" I asked. "And where do you live?"

"My name is Ivory. I live in unit F3."

On Monday evening, I located Ivory and learned she was originally from Brooklyn, New York. She had been at Coleman for eighteen months, and her release was scheduled for September 2015, completing her nine-year sentence. Ivory was a true worshiper who loved the Lord and had the gift "to see in the Spirit." She even said she undergirded me "like Aaron did for Moses" when Moses lacked the strength to carry on.

"Something about you stood out," Ivory said about first seeing me on the compound. She knew in her heart that we would connect.

Ivory laughed as she explained how I had interfered with her worship on the day she first asked me about my book. My face kept appearing in her mind as she prayed earlier that morning and appeared many times before God told her to ask me for the title of my book. She admitted that she was reluctant to ask me about it at first, but because she was obedient, she did as the Lord instructed. She was relieved but not surprised to learn that I was indeed writing a book. God told her to pray for me.

The morning after Ivory had first approached me and again while worshiping, my face appeared in her mind. "Your face was actually becoming rather annoying," she said. But soon after, God told her to tell me that my book would become a bestseller.

I could not help but think back to January 2009 when I pled guilty in federal court. Before the judge announced his verdict, he told me about a man he had sentenced who went on to write a successful book. As I waited for him to decide my fate, I wondered, *Why in the world is he telling this story?*

While I was getting to know my new friend, Ivory, I received in the mail a devotion written by A. J. Russell from his book *God Calling*. It contained a powerful reading entitled "Claim Big Things," which read:

> Listen, listen I am your Lord. Before Me, there is none other. Just trust me in everything. Help is here all the time. The difficult way is nearly over, but you have learned lessons you could learn in no other way. "The Kingdom of Heaven suffered violence, and it is the violent who take it by force." Wrest from Me, by firm and simple trust and persistent prayer, the treasure of My Kingdom.
>
> Such wonderful things are coming to you, Joy—Peace—Assurance—Security—Health—Happiness—Laughter.

Claim big, really big things now. Remember nothing is too big. Satisfy the longing of My Heart to give.[10]

God wants us to trust him, and if he wanted me to claim big things, then that's exactly what I would do. He had already taught me so much and prepared me for my assignment, and he promised to help me every step of the way.

Chapter 8

Most days in prison started off much the same way—before sunrise. With one hundred fifty inmates getting ready each morning, the noise alone would wake us. A good number of inmates needed to wake by six and stand in the "pill line" for their daily medications, and if we wanted to eat breakfast or drop off our laundry, those tasks had to be completed by seven. We also had to make our beds, and most inmates started their jobs between 7:30 and 8:00 a.m.

I worked the second lunch and dinner shifts in the kitchen, which meant my mornings were open. After breakfast, the first thing I did was my Bible study. One Friday morning, I stood by my locker reading my Bible and taking notes. A young woman from down the hall stopped and asked what I was doing.

"I'm reading the Bible and waiting for God to give me direction about what to do next," I replied.

"What do you mean?" she asked.

"I try to keep a pretty low profile, but when God asks me to do something, I do it." I went on to share with her a couple of examples, like the time God told me to write a thank-you note to someone for their kindness and how he sometimes tells me to pray for specific people.

"Well, if God talks to you about me," she said, "come down to 406 and let me know."

I did not know this young woman's name, but I'd talk to her in passing, and she started to warm up to me. As I got to know her, it became clear that she was running with the wrong crowd. They got into verbal altercations with the guards so regularly that the guards learned their names, which wasn't a good thing, and the group leader was loud, obnoxious, and a textbook bully. I mostly avoided them for those reasons, but I also felt compassion for them because people who act out are usually wounded and hurting.

Despite the young woman's worrisome company and rough exterior, I believed that with a little tender loving care, I might eventually convince her to go to church with me. I hoped to show her another side of life that was available to her too. God continued to lay her on my heart, which meant I needed to continue reaching out to her. I went for a walk on the track outside and asked God to reveal something to me about her that no one else would know. That way, she'd know the information had to have come directly from him.

I prayed in the Spirit as I walked around the track, raising my hands in excitement or clenching my fist like I'd just won something or completed a difficult task. The thought of telling this young woman something about herself was as exciting as making a game-winning shot at the buzzer (I played basketball for a long time and still love the sport). I practically danced around the track waiting for God to fulfill this special request.

On the same afternoon that I prayed to God for information about the young woman, I heard a name pop into my head. Then I heard a message. I kind of dismissed it and figured that if it were God, he would tell me these things again since I specifically asked him for a God-slap. A *God-slap* is whenever God wakes you up from a nap or during the night, and you know with 100 percent certainty that he wants to talk to you.

"Don't let me miss it," I told him. "It's important I get this right."

Well, guess who was awakened with a God-slap after a fifteen-minute power nap the next day? I heard the same name and the same message as I had the day before.

It was time to visit cell 406 and find this young woman. She was not in her room, but I found her in the hallway near the bathroom.

"You are not going to believe it," I said. "I asked God to reveal something to me about you that no one else would know." I read the skepticism on her face but continued, "Does the name Tyrone mean anything to you? And is he home alone or all alone?"

Her eyes grew as big as saucers, and she was speechless for a moment. "Katie," she said, "Tyrone is my brother, and he's in prison."

I could only say, "Wow! God told me!" Then I asked, "Is there anything you want me to pray about?"

"Yeah," she said. "Tell God to get me the hell out of here."

The following week, we were talking in her room, and she told me her real name was Shawnitralla, but everyone called her Shawn.

"I still can't believe you knew about Tyrone," she said, shaking her head in disbelief. "No one here knows about Tyrone. No one."

"I have to admit that word of knowledge even surprised me," I confessed, "but I wanted you to know it came directly from God."

I was finding that the more time I spent with the Lord, the more often I would hear from him. It didn't surprise me when a familiar verse rose up in my Spirit when I was relaxing in my room later: "Always be joyful. Never stop praying. Be thankful in all circumstances, for this is God's will for you who belong to Christ Jesus" (1 Thessalonians 5:16–18).

Joy seemed to be the theme of the week. Merriam-Webster's dictionary defines *joy* as "a state of happiness; a source or cause of delight." I wondered, *Are joy and happiness the same thing?*

My question reminded me of an experience I'd had a few years prior during my earlier days of studying the Bible. In a group, I was asked to provide my biblical perspective on happiness. At the time, I had just finished reading *Secrets of a Satisfying Life: Discover the Habits of Happy People,* a book by David Ireland that provided insight into the subject of happiness. I took two important notes from this book. First, true happiness has very little to do with circumstances and has more to do with perspective, and second, satisfaction can be learned. A Bible verse that supports this was written by the apostle Paul: "Not that I was ever in need, for I have learned how to be content with whatever I have. I know how to live on almost nothing or with everything. I have learned the secret of living in every situation, whether it is with a full stomach or empty, with plenty or little" (Philippians 4:11–12).

The book of Ecclesiastes provides additional wisdom on happiness. Solomon, a king of Israel who enjoyed a close relationship with God and is considered by many to be the wisest man who ever lived, said, "I decided there is nothing better than to enjoy food and drink and to find satisfaction in work. Then I realized these pleasures are from God" (2:24). According to Solomon, then, happiness is a choice.

We find happiness in the measure of satisfaction that we see in life's normal, everyday activities. Some would argue that prison is not normal, but I would argue that for the inmates living this life, it is normal and that the promises of the Bible are for everyone, including inmates. Each of us can choose to be happy in our present circumstances, no matter what those circumstances are. Happiness is not as elusive as many people think.

Joy, on the other hand, is a bit different. It was actually one of the constant and dominant themes of Mother Teresa's ministry. Mother Teresa was a Catholic nun who was officially declared a saint by the Catholic church. She was born in 1910, and in 1946, she experienced what she described as "the call within the call" when she felt God leading her to go on a retreat in Calcutta. She began her missionary work with the poor in 1948, focusing on helping those who were dying of diseases like HIV, AIDS, leprosy, and tuberculosis. She often said that the best way to show our gratitude to others is to do everything with joy. She described joy as the fruit of the Holy Spirit and a characteristic mark of the kingdom of God, for God is joy.[11] Joy is a sign of generosity, as well as intimate and constant union with God.

Most people associate the word *intimacy* with sex, but in Christianity, *intimacy* means relating to God on emotional and spiritual levels. To be intimate with God means you have a genuine fellowship, or relationship, with him. If that sounds intimidating, remember that the Lord created humans in his image so that all people could relate to him and enjoy a relationship with him. The Holy Spirit lives within every believer, too, allowing us to develop a personal friendship with Christ.

However, intimacy cannot exist without trust. If we refuse to obey and surrender to God, we can't expect to have an intimate relationship with him. Oneness with God must be motivated out of love, not duty. We don't have to earn his affection. God forgave each one of us for all our sins when Christ died on the cross. Let that truth motivate you to freely and genuinely devote yourself to getting to know God better so that you can experience the fullness of friendship with him. Be honest with him, and intimacy will grow.

One of the best parts about having a solid relationship with the Lord is that he becomes an anchor for us during life's storms, assuring us that he is always with us and ready to help in any situation or circumstance. We can embrace true peace in our spirit because we know he will guide us every step of the way.

My reflecting on joy and peace also got me thinking about hope. Hope is the anchor of the soul, and it's synonymous with optimism and courage. In fact, the Bible defines *hope* as "confident expectation" (2 Corinthians 1:7 AMP). Christian hope is rooted in our faith in Jesus Christ, and our relationship with him offers us hope.

Hope changes the way we see ourselves, what we value, and what we do with our lives. Through the power of the Holy Spirit, hope produces joy and peace in believers, and it provides protection, strength, courage, and confidence every day. Hope in God's Word, hope in God's promises, and hope in God's grace give us the comfort and assurance we need on this journey.

There's a walking path at Coleman that hundreds of inmates call the Path of Hope. It's one-third of a mile long and made up of crushed seashells and small stones. Every day, inmates head to the path to exercise, pray, reflect on life, and find hope to endure their remaining time in prison.

When we walked or ran around the path, we hoped for lots of things—that our families were well taken care of, that we might be released early, and that the truth of our respective cases would someday be known. We hoped our prayers would be answered, and we hoped we could find the strength to carry on. While on that path, I'd hear people sing Christian songs, see them give each other hugs, and shed tears. People's lives changed on that path thanks to hope. Zechariah said, "Come back to the place of safety, all you prisoners who still have hope! I promise this very day that I will repay two blessings for each of your troubles" (9:12).

And we certainly had troubles. One day was particularly tough. It started like most Sundays. I was watching a televised sermon by famous minister Charles Stanley, and he was reminding viewers that we must praise God when we suffer. It's no one's instinct to do so, of course, but through suffering, we grow and mature. Through suffering, we are conformed to Christ's image, and through praise and thanksgiving, we learn to trust God.

After the program, I grabbed a cup of coffee and headed to the Path of Hope for some exercise. My walk was cut short, though, when I ran into Carol, whose face showed a look of despair.

"Go get the others," Carol said with urgency. "We need to pray. Anabel's son was murdered this morning." Anabel was Carol's roommate.

Without another word, I sprinted to the unit and found most of the twelve members of our small Bible study group. While Anabel sat with the chaplain, we gathered on the racquetball court, hand in hand, and prayed. Some prayers were spoken in English, some in Spanish, and others were spoken in our respective prayer languages. After approximately twenty minutes, a quiet peace enveloped us. Then a few of the ladies returned to the chapel to wait for Anabel. I felt compelled to continue to pray.

I walked toward the bleachers near the softball diamond and wondered how we would help Anabel survive the loss of her child. But before I even sat on the bleachers, I was overcome by God's presence. I continued to cry, and I thought of the sermon I'd watched that morning. I remembered to worship, praise, and thank the Lord even though this was a tragedy and every parent's worst nightmare.

I sat on the bleachers and wept, and then I watched Anabel, Carol, and the other ladies walk slowly out of the chapel with their arms around each other. In that moment, I witnessed an outpouring of love and unity that only God could orchestrate. Countless hearts were moved that day as evidenced by the compassion shown to Anabel. She put one foot in front of the other while the ladies led her back to her unit. I almost didn't notice they were walking on the Path of Hope.

I sat behind Anabel and Carol while we waited for the two o'clock church service to begin. Most Sundays, gospel music, heavenly singing, and festive praise filled the chapel. People even smiled. But the news of Anabel's son left a heavy somberness in the air, and I knew our worship that day would be far different from our usual services.

Dabbing my tears, I asked God why. *Why does it have to be this way, Lord? I know you work all things together for good, but isn't there enough hurt here? How can a mother possibly endure the loss of her twenty-three-year-old son while she's in prison?* I did not receive an answer that day but understood that my job was to trust God and persevere in prayer.

I prayed that God would give Anabel and her family the strength to carry on. I prayed for justice to be served. I prayed that her family would be able to find forgiveness. I prayed for healing and peace. I prayed for Anabel to not give up, and I prayed for Carol to find the right words to comfort Anabel that night and in the days ahead.

We wonder why God allows bad things to happen, and we question or doubt his goodness without seeing the full picture. In reality, God does not have to answer to anyone for what he does or doesn't do. And things take place behind the scenes that we know nothing about. That's why we have to trust God under all circumstances. Jesus tells us to trust God not only when we do not understand but *because* we do not understand (Proverbs 3:5–6). We may never know the specific reason for our suffering, but we must trust God, whose ways are perfect.

Suffering obviously comes with being incarcerated, and on days like the one when we received the news of Anabel's son, it was even more painful to be inside Coleman. But, as God had told my friend Paula, the final chapter needed to be written. And interestingly enough, God confirmed his message on Mother's Day weekend while I was talking to an inmate who lived next door.

We were waiting for the ten o'clock head count when she received a prompting from the Holy Spirit about my journey: "You are on a mission. You will be here until you finish the book completely. Then you will be ready to face what is next. Be at peace."

From a biblical standpoint, the word *mission* is the divine activity of sending intermediaries to speak or do God's will so that his purposes are fulfilled. It means to be sent like the apostles in the time of Jesus. Apostles are divinely commissioned messengers of the good news. I guess that explains why God led me to the following passage in which King David spoke to Solomon: "Worship and serve [God] with your whole heart and a willing mind. For the LORD sees every heart and knows every plan and thought. If you seek him, you will find him. But if you forsake him, he will reject you forever. So take this seriously. The LORD has chosen you…Be strong, and do the work" (1 Chronicles 28:9–10).

When God tells me to take something seriously, I do. And he was giving me a very specific, interesting instruction: "Pray for your release."

Pray for my release? I thought. That didn't make sense. But if I knew anything by this point, it was that God's thoughts are not my thoughts, and his ways are far beyond anything I could ever imagine. God is in the miracle business, so if he wanted me to pray for my release, then that was exactly what I would do.

Some inmates heard rumors that Coleman was going to be turned into a men's facility and prison camps would no longer be funded, given the expense of incarcerating nonviolent offenders. That information gave me hope that an early release was in the works. I was eager to share this latest communication with my Bible study group, as I sensed in my spirit that they would also be involved in praying for my release.

It did not take God long to impress upon my heart what was next. I was to ask Paula to invite some of my friends to her home in Tampa for an evening of prayer on Tuesday, May 15. Both Paula and I hear from the Lord, so she did not hesitate to arrange the gathering. Prayer was to begin at seven, and those who attended would be anointed with oil. With the lights dimmed, candles lit, and music playing in the background, the room would usher in the Holy Spirit while everyone prayed for me and my release. The group was to keep praying on their knees until peace washed over them. I was to pray on my knees in my room at the exact same time.

Shortly before seven o'clock on the evening of Tuesday, May 15, I got on my knees and began to pray. In Tampa, the group prayed for the Holy Spirit to enter Paula's home and fill them to overflowing. These ladies worshiped on their knees. Some wept, and some prayed in their prayer languages.

Peace eventually fell over the room. The group continued in prayer, and it wasn't until the music ended that they resumed conversation. My friends then shared what God had spoken to their hearts and what they were feeling. Paula believed everyone was touched by the hand of God.

"Many witnessed about your joy in the midst of your situation and the number of lives being touched by your faith in your Father God," Paula shared with me. "It was a beautiful evening of peace as we prayed for you, my dear sister. Thank you for your obedience to

God. We will now wait to see the manifest workings of God brought about by this prayer agreement."

I saw Paula and Diana on a Sunday over Memorial Day weekend just days after my fifty-fifth birthday on May 24. The first thing Diana asked during their visit was whether 5:19 meant anything to me. The sound of an alarm had awakened her at precisely that hour and minute the morning prior, but she didn't keep an alarm in her room. She chalked it up to the Lord because she felt strongly these numbers were for me.

When I told them I was born at 5:19 in the evening, they couldn't believe it. My spirit sensed that I needed to read every fifth chapter and nineteenth verse in the Bible. I was convinced I would find some sort of personal message in one of these verses.

Guess what I found in the book of Galatians? "When you follow the desires of your sinful nature, the results are very clear: sexual immorality, impurity, lustful pleasures" (5:19). The list continues, but it begins with sexual immorality. Unfortunately, this type of moral impurity makes fellowship with God impossible. We must confront our sinful desires if we want to follow the Holy Spirit's guidance.

Galatians 5:19 also relates to Galatians 5:24, and May 24 is my birthday. Galatians 5:24 says, "Those who belong to Christ Jesus have nailed the passions and desires of their sinful nature to his cross and crucified them there." The date and time of my birth corresponded with my spiritual rebirth. *Unbelievable!* I thought.

A few days later, I stood on the top of the bleachers, spread out my arms in prayer, and cried out at the top of my lungs, "Lord, come get me!" I wanted out of Coleman, and I believed, like the apostles, that God would miraculously open that door to freedom.

That very night, God woke me from my sleep and spoke the following words: *Come away, my beloved.* I was processing God's words when, all of a sudden, it hit me: God had just proposed to me. It wasn't a literal marriage proposal but a spiritual one.

Yes, Lord, I replied. *I'm all in.*

The same words I heard God speak are found in the Bible in the Song of Solomon, also known as the Song of Songs, which is a book in the Old Testament penned by Solomon. It's written in the form of romantic poetry and reads like a passionate conversation between a bride and her bridegroom, which means the same thing as a groom or a man who's about to be married.

The verse I heard God speak was from 2:10, in which the bride recognizes her groom's voice when he says, "Rise up, my darling! Come away with me, my fair one!" He says it again in 2:13, and he repeats himself because of his overwhelming desire to be with the bride he loves. He goes on to tell her who she is in him and affirms her beauty, thus celebrating their love.

In his kindness, the bridegroom invites his bride to come away with him so that he can lavish her with love, show her who he is, and speak his desires into her heart, which is exactly what God had been doing since the day I arrived at Coleman.

Just before I fell back to sleep, I asked God to reveal when I would leave Coleman. He simply told me to look up the word *come*. So, like a good student, I went to the subject index at the back of my Bible and found only one verse listed: Revelation 22:17. This verse reads, "The Spirit and the bride say, 'Come.' Let anyone who hears this say, 'Come.' Let anyone who is thirsty come. Let anyone who desires drink freely from the water of life." The verse also relates to Revelation 22:20: "He who is the faithful witness to all these things says, 'Yes, I am coming soon!'"

I began to wonder. Could I figure out from these verses what day I would be released? It was June 1 when God proposed to me, so I started to read all the 6:1 Bible verses I could find. First Samuel 6:1 was among the first ones I read: "The Ark of the LORD remained in Philistine territory seven months in all."

Hmm, I thought. *What other numbers in the Bible are meaningful?*

The number forty is mentioned hundreds of times, and it's a number of great significance. It rained forty days and nights when

God flooded the earth (Genesis 7:12). Not once but twice was Moses on a mountain with God for forty days and forty nights (Exodus 24:18, 34:28–29; Deuteronomy 10:10). The Israelites wandered in the wilderness for forty years (Exodus 16:35; Numbers 14:33–34). Jesus fasted in the wilderness for forty days (Matthew 4:1–2) and was seen on the earth for forty days after his crucifixion (Acts 1:3). A forty-something period of time, be it days or years, is always a period of testing or trial that ends with restoration, revival, or renewal.

I calculated forty days from June 1: July 11. That was seven months and seven days from the day I walked into Coleman. In the Bible, the number seven represents completion and perfection. Did that mean I would complete my time on July 11? Only God knew.

The date of July 11 would not leave my mind, so I asked God if I would be released that day. He sent me to every 7:11 Bible verse I could find. Here's what I found in the book of Isaiah: "Ask the LORD your God for a sign of confirmation…Make it as difficult as you want—as high as heaven or as deep as the place of the dead" (7:11).

Okay, Lord, I need one more confirmation, I said. *I need to feel your presence.*

He then asked me, *What day were you sentenced?*

My sentencing was on November 23, and Numbers 11:23 reads, "The LORD said to Moses, 'Has my arm lost its power? Now you will see whether or not my word comes true!'" And in Mark 11:23, Jesus said, "You can say to this mountain, 'May you be lifted up and thrown into the sea,' and it will happen. But you must really believe it will happen and have no doubt in your heart."

I shared my studies of biblical numbers with another inmate, and she told me the Holy Spirit had given her advice about me: *Stay close to her*, the Lord told her. *She is blessed and faithful.*

"He sees your heart, Katie. Everything you ask for will come to you."

I prayed to the Lord that I would be released on July 11. Within a few days of that prayer, I received an email from Paula telling me the Lord had directed her to a passage in Romans.

Abraham never wavered in believing God's promise. In fact, his faith grew stronger, and in this he brought glory to God. He was fully convinced that God is able to do whatever he promises. And because of Abraham's faith, God counted him as righteous. And when God counted him as righteous, it wasn't just for Abraham's benefit. It was recorded for our benefit, too, assuring us that God will also count us as righteous if we believe in him, the one who raised Jesus our Lord from the dead. He was handed over to die because of our sins, and he was raised to life to make us right with God. (4:20–25)

This passage made it clear that God had much to teach my spiritual support team, which included my Bible study group, church members, friends, and family. They were encouraged by the emails I'd been sending them from prison. My life became a living, breathing testament to God's goodness and grace, and he wanted my team to call out on my behalf and seek his face.

One of the other verses God stressed that we study was Romans 4:17, which reads a little bit differently in the King James Version of the Bible. It says, "Calleth those things which be not as though they were." We are to call what is not as though it already is. In other words, God wanted us to begin to speak of my July release as though it had already happened.

Then, while showering one afternoon, God told me, *The answer you are looking for is in two seventeen*. I read all the 2:17 verses in the Bible, and they were reminiscent of my past life—full of warnings related to sexual immorality, pride, and idolatry. But unfortunately, I still couldn't figure out what God was trying to tell me.

On July 10, I received a vision. It was as if I were standing in the driveway of my townhome in Tampa, looking at the house's number: 4916. Once again, I grabbed my Bible and camped out in Isaiah 49 since it's one of the few books in the Bible with forty-nine chapters. I found a section entitled "The Lord's Servant Commissioned," and verse 16 says, "See, I have written your name on the palms of my hands."

I was not sure what God was up to, but I knew it was good.

Chapter 9

I woke up on July 11, brimming with excitement and hoping to be released early. My excitement continued to build as the day progressed. Many women offered me encouraging words. They, too, felt confident I would be set free. Other women looked at me like I was nuts, convinced I had lost my mind.

Then the unexpected happened. While serving lunch, I watched two panicked officers sprint toward the cafeteria doors and slam them shut. We were in lockdown. Nearly three hundred women sat in the cafeteria, and chaos erupted. People stood up in their seats and ran to the windows, trying to figure out what was happening. Did someone escape? Was there a medical emergency?

All of a sudden, an incredible storm appeared out of nowhere. Ferocious winds swirled around dark clouds, and trees bent in submission, their leaves and branches whipping off. Heavy rain lashed at the roof. All hell broke loose outside, signaling to me that a fierce battle was underway in the spiritual realm.

"Something is happening," a woman said to me. "I think you're going home!" Another woman gave me a thumbs-up.

I had to tell Carol, so I walked into the dish room. "Don't be surprised if we see a cross in the middle of the infield and God picks me up in a chariot," I told Carol, who nodded in agreement. She always said she wanted a cross placed in the middle of the infield.

Then it hit me: *What if this place gets leveled to the ground and God really does bring me home?*

After close to an hour, the winds subsided, the dark clouds receded, and the downpour of rain came to an end. The officers gave the all-clear, and everyone continued with their afternoon.

I returned to the unit, took a shower, and waited expectantly for my name to be called. If you were going to be released, you would be called to the message center, which is a building that houses the administrative team. It was the one place you did not want to be called to unless you had a weekend visitor. Otherwise, it usually meant something bad had happened or was about to happen. It could also mean a random drug test or a transfer.

Interestingly, I had been called to the message center the night before, and everyone, including myself, believed I was going home. It turned out I had been called for a random drug test, and when I returned to my unit, many people encouraged me that the call was simply a "practice run" for the next day.

But time passed, and my name wasn't called, which meant it was time for me to head back to work in the kitchen.

At 4:25 p.m., the Holy Spirit rose up inside of me, and I began praying.

"God is up to something," I told a coworker, "and he is serious."

I stood at a window near the back of the cafeteria and watched another fierce storm roll in. I closed my eyes and prayed in tongues. My hands opened, my arms extended away from my body, and my head lifted toward heaven.

About ten minutes later, I sensed someone near me. I opened my eyes and looked to my right. Dale, a woman from the dish room, stood a few tables away from me. After glancing at her, I closed my eyes and continued to pray.

The following story is from Dale's perspective. Within days of this event, I asked her to record her experience.

That day in the kitchen when you were by the window, praying and watching the storm come in, I was walking around behind you and praying myself. Well, the Lord kept pressing upon me to lay my hands on your shoulders…I finally gave in…As soon as I touched you on the shoulders, I knew it was God because it felt like a surge or electrical shock was running down my arms and hands and into you. It was like no one was around but me and you. Time stood still.

Dale also said that when she touched me, she began to speak her prayer language, which rarely occurs for her.

I hadn't sensed Dale behind me, but when she touched me, my knees buckled. Not only did I feel the same power surge that she described, but I also felt an incredible anointing. Just one day before, God had led me to Isaiah 49:16: "I have written your name on the palms of my hands." Dale had placed the palms of her hands on my shoulders. I believe that was the moment I was commissioned as a faithful witness to God's purposes.

Through tears, I prayed near the window for another five minutes. It was one of the most intense prayers I'd ever prayed. At one point, I spoke the word *obedience* in my prayer language. Biblical obedience is submitting to God's authority and trusting him, and I had given him my entire heart over the last forty days. That may be why he told me at seven that morning, *Now you will see whether or not my word comes true.* God had spoken to Paula at the exact same time that morning, telling her not once but twice, *Let those who doubt, doubt no more.*

By bedtime, I still hadn't been called to the message center. Obviously, I was disappointed because I was certain of what God had told me. I thought I had clearly heard him say that I would be released on July 11. My prayer team in Tampa was even on standby to pick me up. I was ready to go, but his timing was not mine. I took a deep breath and wondered what I had missed. Although, according to Isaiah 60:22, I might not have missed anything: "At the right time, I, the LORD, will make it happen."

During breakfast the next morning, I mentioned to my friends that God had me all stirred up about 2:17 again. If you recall, he had told me a few days earlier that the answer I was looking for was in two seventeen, so I had read all the 2:17 verses in the Bible but could not yet make sense of what he was trying to tell me.

I went outside an hour or so later and sat on a picnic bench. I ended up sharing my story about 2:17 with a woman sitting next to me.

"You need to go to F2," she said, which was the unit she lived in. She returned to her unit to see who lived in cell 217 and relayed my message to the women inhabiting it that I hoped to speak with them.

After lunch, I entered F2. I should first note that I could have gotten into big trouble for entering their unit, as that was a no-no. But I asked God to protect me so that I wouldn't run into a guard, counselor, or case manager. I reached cell 217 and entered, not knowing what to expect.

The women's names were Crystal and Jackie. I did not know their stories; we seldom did since few inmates ever talked about their crimes. Quite frankly, their crimes didn't matter. I just saw two women in the same boat as me, and I knew in my heart that one of them held the answer I was looking for.

I started off the conversation by introducing myself. Then I said, "I have no idea why I'm here, but the Lord does. Please just start talking to me and tell me a little bit about yourself and your life, and I'll see if I can figure out what God is trying to tell me."

As we talked, it became apparent that Jackie and I had a lot in common, primarily that neither of us felt loved. Jackie was given up for adoption and struggled with feelings of rejection. And while I used material possessions, work accomplishments, and inappropriate sexual relationships to distract me from my loneliness, Jackie filled her void with food. Her relationship with food and overeating was an ongoing battle. She also spoke about her separation from her husband, who later fell sick.

"I took my marriage vows seriously," she said. "I went back and took care of him until he died. That was twelve years ago."

Now I knew which Bible verse God meant for me to understand: "Wisdom will save you from the immoral woman, from the seductive words of the promiscuous woman. She has abandoned her husband and ignores the covenant she made before God" (Proverbs 2:16–17). This Scripture touches on two of the most difficult sins to resist: sexual immorality and pride. By sleeping with men who are not her husband, a woman is sexually immoral. By abandoning her husband and ignoring the vows she made before God, she is prideful. Whereas pride says, "I deserve it," sexual desire says, "I need it." When combined, their appeal is deadly.

Pride appeals to an empty head, which means thinking about yourself and your feelings without thought, care, or consideration for how your decisions impact others. Sexual enticement, on the other hand, appeals to an empty heart. But only God can fill our heads with wisdom and our hearts with love. That's why we must rely on his strength to overcome these sins.[12] But even when we fail, he still loves us. Let's read the Bible story of the woman caught in adultery.

> Jesus returned to the Mount of Olives, but early the next morning he was back again at the Temple. A crowd soon gathered, and he sat down and taught them. As he was speaking, the teachers of religious law and the Pharisees brought a woman who had been caught in the act of adultery. They put her in front of the crowd.
>
> "Teacher," they said to Jesus, "this woman was caught in the act of adultery. The law of Moses says to stone her. What do you say?"
>
> They were trying to trap him into saying something they could use against him, but Jesus stooped down and wrote in the dust with his finger. They kept demanding an answer, so he stood up again and said, "All right, but let the one who has never sinned throw the first stone!" Then he stooped down again and wrote in the dust.

When the accusers heard this, they slipped away one by one, beginning with the oldest, until only Jesus was left in the middle of the crowd with the woman. Then Jesus stood up again and said to the woman, "Where are your accusers? Didn't even one of them condemn you?"

"No, Lord," she said.

And Jesus said, "Neither do I. Go and sin no more." (John 8:1–12)

God is willing to give us a second chance, but a new life in Christ means we must have a change of heart. We cannot keep chasing after the things of this world and feeding our fleshy desires. As John wrote,

Do not love this world nor the things it offers you, for when you love the world, you do not have the love of the Father in you. For the world offers only a craving for physical pleasure, a craving for everything we see, and pride in our achievements and possessions. These are not from the Father, but are from this world. And this world is fading away, along with everything that people crave. But anyone who does what pleases God will live forever. (1 John 2:15–17)

God's Word is clear: We must be obedient. His relationship with each of us is characterized by our faithfulness, and he takes the marriage covenant seriously. I couldn't help but wonder if he had been testing me for the last forty days to see if I would obey and honor the commitment I'd made to him on June 1, the day he proposed to me, "Come away, my Beloved!"

How faithful and trustworthy was I during this forty-day courtship and testing period? I obeyed every prompting. Whenever I had an opportunity to share my testimony, I did. Whenever people needed prayer, I prayed. When he insisted that I write about specific, often unusual things in my emails to friends and family (who must have thought I'd lost my mind), I wrote them anyway. When another inmate needed a roommate, I moved in. When God insisted that I give everything away, I did. As a matter of fact, one of the inmates said to me, "You remind me of Abraham. I think you would shave your head if God told you to."

I had done everything God asked me to do. Everything. I followed every one of his instructions and obeyed every one of his promptings. I stepped out in faith and did exactly what he asked of me—because I love him, I trust him, and I choose to be faithful to who he calls me to be.

A verse in the book of Ecclesiastes helped me see faithfulness in a new light too: "God has made everything beautiful for its own time. He has planted eternity in the human heart, but even so, people cannot see the whole scope of God's work from beginning to end" (3:11). By planting eternity in the human heart, God placed a restlessness within us. We will never be completely satisfied here on earth. Whatever we're looking for "more" of can only be found in an intimate relationship with God. That's exactly what he was telling me with Proverbs 2:17: the security I craved would only be found in him.

In early August, I received a court order requesting my appearance in the United States District Court for the Eastern District of Wisconsin to testify at trial. I was scheduled to leave on Tuesday, August 14, 2012, and I arrived at the message center at 5:30 that morning to find a rather imposing male officer carrying three sets of handcuffs and shackles. One set was for me, and the other two were for women who also had court appearances that day. A female officer was with us, too, and the embroidered patch on her jacket told me she was a member of the crisis support team.

The officers told the three of us to wait outside of the message center. One of the girls was throwing up. *Great*, I thought. Before leaving, the female officer strip-searched us, and we changed into traveling clothes, which consisted of a brown T-shirt, khaki-colored elastic waist pants, and blue slip-on tennis shoes.

For the first time, I felt like a prisoner. A tightly pulled chain wrapped around my waist, and with the handcuffs on, I could only move my hands a few inches in any direction. The ankle cuffs were just as uncomfortable. I had been able to laugh off many of the things that happened to me at Coleman so far, but this was no laughing matter.

At 7:15 the officers led us to a van. The restraints made it so difficult to walk and move that I needed help getting inside the vehicle. I chose the back seat since both of the other girls were now carrying barf bags. We were taken to another facility to be processed, and then it was back to the van to return to Coleman and wait for two buses of male prisoners to be transferred. *It's going to be a long day*, I thought.

We finally departed Coleman a little after 10:00 a.m. to head toward Tampa International Airport. But shortly after getting on the road, the officers took one of the first exits off the interstate. I was surprised when we pulled into a McDonald's parking lot. *Guess the officers need to eat too*, I thought. It did seem like a good time to eat, so I opened my lunch bag. I ate the cookies and the bag of chips but mostly gave up on having a sandwich. How in the world is a person wearing handcuffs supposed to make a peanut butter and jelly sandwich?

The vehicles headed south, and I was happy to see my old stomping grounds: The Grove Shopping Center, the International Mall, Raymond James Stadium, where the Tampa Bay Buccaneers play, and so many familiar roads and exits.

A little after eleven, we drove onto the airport property and were given a restroom break. I was so dehydrated that I could not urinate, so I found a drinking fountain and drank as much water as I could.

By this time, I had a headache. Rap music had been blaring in the van all morning, and I was tired from having to wake up early. At 12:30 a lieutenant approached the van, called my last name, and said, "Receiving and Discharge just called. The written order of the court has been canceled. You're going back to Coleman with us."

Step Into Prison, Step Out in Faith

You have got to be kidding me, I thought to myself. What in the world was God up to?

The plane arrived a little after three, and the transfer process took two hours. Inmates being transferred to Coleman had to move from the plane to the bus, and those being transferred out of Coleman had to shuffle from the bus to the plane. Armed guards sealed off the perimeter. Watching everything unfold made me feel like I was watching a movie.

While waiting inside the van, I saw the devil over and over again. Scary-looking people: unblinking eyes, shaved heads or unkempt hair, pronounced scars, tattoos of the grim reaper, skeletons, or images of hell. Some had teardrop tattoos on their faces, which is a common symbol in prison and gang cultures that typically means a person has killed someone. You could feel the intensity of their anger in the atmosphere. I was thankful the doors were locked.

I felt safe until both officers exited the van to attend to the prisoners outside. But first they turned off the van's engine. The temperature was in the mid-nineties, the sun beat down on the windows, and only one was cracked open about four inches. I was chained and shackled and hadn't had anything to drink for hours.

Not only was sweat pouring off me, but I was also starting to feel claustrophobic. I know how quickly a temperature can reach 160 degrees inside a vehicle, so I knocked on the window and asked an officer to please turn on the air conditioning. He said no. After another ten to fifteen minutes, the officers returned to the vehicle, but the engine wouldn't turn over. The battery was dead. They finally slid open the side doors of the van so that I could get some air, and I welcomed the ninety-five-degree breeze, relieved I did not suffer the same fate as the battery.

We were back on the road shortly after 5:30 in the evening, and I settled in for the ride by answering questions posed to me by the new inmates transferred from other federal facilities. After I had worn the shackles for twelve hours, a guard finally removed them from my wrists and ankles. One more strip search and I'd be free to return to the compound at Coleman. I grabbed the few personal items I'd left behind: a gray T-shirt, a pair of Russell brand shorts that I had purchased from the commissary, and a pair of flip-flops that also served as my shower shoes. It wasn't much, but it was all I needed to feel like I was back where I belonged.

All the remaining puzzle pieces came together. As I was walking the track later that week, I received the release I had been waiting for. God spoke three words to me: *chains of addiction.* I had to smile because the Holy Spirit had put a book in my hands a few days earlier called *Codependent No More.*

How do you know when you have finally broken the chains of addiction? Joyce Meyer may have said it best in her book *Managing Your Emotions:*

> Freedom from codependency is based upon the development of a sense of value apart from what a person does. If you are free from codependency, you are not dependent on people, places, or positions. You don't have to be in a relationship with any certain person or group of people, or to be in a certain place, or occupy a certain position to feel safe, confident, and secure.
>
> If you are free from codependency, you don't feel you have to be in control of everything and everybody. You can allow others to make their own choices and not feel threatened or responsible for them. You don't feel you have to solve every problem or satisfy every person.[13]

The chains I had to wear represented my past, my sexual codependency, and all my other sins that would have prevented me from inheriting the kingdom of heaven. Thankfully, I had nailed them to the cross and crucified my sinful desires: pride, sexual immorality, impurity, and lustful pleasures. It was no longer I who live but Christ who lives in me.

Dale was ironing her clothes when the Holy Spirit told her to find me. She went outside to see if I was on the track, and because she did not see me there, she returned to pressing her uniform. God told her again to find me, so she finished up and said, *God, if this is of you, then when I walk back outside, I want Katie to be there.* And I was.

Dale heard me talking to another inmate and called my name, so I met her on the sidewalk between our units. As she walked toward me, she said God instructed her to bless and anoint me in the name of the Father, Son, and Holy Spirit. She felt she was supposed to hold my hands and pray a quick prayer, so she did. Then we talked for a few minutes before parting ways.

When Dale returned to her room, however, she received additional marching orders from God. He told her to pray with me again, but this time she was to place a cross on my forehead in the name of the Father, a cross on my right palm in the name of the Son, and a cross on my left palm in the name of the Holy Spirit. Dale found me in my room and did as she was instructed.

Dale said, "This is what God told me to say: 'Satan, you cannot have her. She belongs to me.' Katie, you are his, and I plead the shed blood of Jesus over you." To plead the blood of Jesus over someone means you are declaring the power of Jesus over Satan and his schemes.

I did not know what to say, so I hugged Dale and thanked her. While hugging, Dale began to speak in tongues and was so overcome by the power of the Holy Spirit that she could hardly stand. I held her up as we embraced. Dale was crying, and we both felt such incredible, profound joy. I felt like I was walking on cloud nine.

When we let go of each other, I jumped up and down, spun around, and said, "Did you hear that? God said Satan can't have me. I am his!" I hugged her again, knowing we had just experienced a miracle.

"You will do awesome work with children, and God is going to send one special child your way."

A few weeks later, Dale appeared in my dream. In it, she brought me a piece of paper with an organizational chart drawn on it and twenty-five names. My name was the first on the list. Dale told me I was smart and to take care of the other people on the list and buy each of them a computer. I woke from the dream feeling like God had given me my marching orders.

The next morning, I was showering when I heard the Spirit speak to my heart. God told me I had proven myself trustworthy and revealed that the organizational chart from my dream was the structure for the nonprofit organization I would later start: The Vivian Foundation. After my shower, I headed to F3 to tell Dale about my dream.

Before I could say anything, Dale asked, "God sent you over here, didn't he?"

"Yes," I said. She smiled.

"We need to talk." Dale went on to tell me that the Spirit had spoken to her during the night too. She told God she would wait for me to come to her to deliver his last message since she was being released the following day for having completed her sentence. Keep in mind that I had never shared with Dale how long I had been on my spiritual journey.

Dale said that God called me his pearl and had been refining and polishing me for the last eight years, conforming me to his image. To fully understand the meaning of this message, we need to know the parable of the pearl in Matthew 13:45–46: "The Kingdom of Heaven is like a merchant on the lookout for choice pearls. When he discovered a pearl of great value, he sold everything he owned and bought it!"

Put simply, the pearl represents those who believe in the kingdom of heaven and those of us who exceed all other treasures in value—so much so that Jesus said everything else should be forfeited to acquire it. God paid the ultimate price to save and redeem us, his pearls, through the death of his only Son.

The symbolism of the pearl struck me in another way too. At least a dozen times while walking the track at Coleman, I had kicked the gravel and thought, *Someday I am going to find a pearl here.* Little did I know the significance of those words.

The second thing God told Dale was that I had to give him something deep inside my heart, something no one else knew about. He said I had buried my pain deep and locked it away for a long time, but he assured Dale he would take care of it. Dale said the source of my pain wasn't for her to know but that I needed to give it to God, and then I could finally have the peace I desperately needed.

I stood silent for a few minutes, completely lost in my thoughts. They drifted to a few places, and when I found the heartache buried inside of me, I felt a gentle nudge toward a specific event, something disturbing that happened to me as a young child. I then prayed to God and asked him to help me through the pain.

Dale's third message from God excited me. Remember how he was going to send me a special child? Well, he revealed more details: *It will be a girl. She's a "spitfire" and has a lot of Katie in her. It's going to take everything Katie has to help her recover from her pain, but Katie will be successful in helping this child on her journey.*

Last, Dale said it was time for one final anointing, and this time it was to be done with prayer oil she bought from the commissary. She dabbed a few drops on my forehead in the name of the Father, a few on my right palm in the name of the Son, and a few on my left palm in the name of the Holy Spirit. With that, God's "pearl" was polished and ready to shine.

Two weeks later, God told me there was still work to be done. Around that same time, I had been walking and praying with a woman down on her luck for over twelve years. After sharing a great day of fellowship with her, I understood that the work the Lord was referring to was my prison ministry. However, what took place the night before his latest message left me in awe of how he works.

Do you remember Shawn? God had revealed to me her brother's name, Tyrone, despite her never mentioning him to any of the inmates. Well, after having been gone for six months, Shawn was back at Coleman. We spoke a bit on the night she returned and shared that she and Tyrone had testified against the other defendants in their case.

Originally, Tyrone had received a ten-year sentence, and after serving fewer than four years, he was released to a halfway house. Shawn was currently awaiting her downward departure. A downward departure is when a federal judge issues a lower sentence than the recommended minimum, and it's often granted for cooperating.

I was catching her up on the goings-on at Coleman when I felt God's presence. Throughout our discussion, I felt in my spirit that Shawn's experience was prophetic in the sense that I, too, would receive a downward departure but hopefully without having to testify. I was almost certain I was hearing the Holy Spirit correctly on this one, but only time would tell.

The strangest part of what happened with Shawn was that she was called to the message center at four o'clock in the afternoon and did not return. I'm not sure if she was released, transferred, or something else. The only thing I knew was that she returned to Coleman for fewer than twenty-four hours and delivered a message from above to me.

I continued to work on my prison ministry to other inmates. One inmate visited me and broke down in tears because her sixteen-year-old son was struggling hard with her imprisonment. He had run away from home, started experimenting with drugs and alcohol, and posted on his Facebook page that he was "lonely and sad." She felt defeated and said, "When I came here, he lost part of his life: me." Another mother had said that being in prison was like death without closure.

Just a few months earlier, there was a real death at Coleman. I had been faced down on the floor in my room, giving praise to God with my friend and fellow inmate, Susan. We were both so grateful for everything God was doing in our lives. Another inmate from our unit, visibly upset, came into my cell and told us, "Miss Mary was down in F3 and unresponsive."

Immediately, Susan and I went to the multipurpose room, where we could see the parking lot and a good portion of the compound. Through the large windows, we saw a rescue squad and a fire truck parked outside. The speed at which the medical staff moved gave away the severity of the situation. Susan, who was a nurse, ran to F3 to offer assistance. We had never seen so many administrators on our compound at one time. Someone counted sixteen.

Chaplains arrived, and in short order, everyone from F3 was called to the visiting room. The remaining inmates were instructed to return to their units. In our hearts, we all understood what had happened, although none of us wanted to speak it or believe it. The women in F3 received the news first, and it did not take long for the rest of the compound to learn of Mary's passing.

It was close to eleven in the morning before the kitchen line servers were called to the cafeteria, almost an hour past our usual time. The air carried a quietness and a sadness that are difficult to explain, and my spirit felt so heavy. The correctional officers called the F1, F2, and F4 units to lunch while the women of F3, still upset and grieving, remained in the visiting room. Most of the inmates had finished eating by the time F3 started to head toward the cafeteria. It was apparent that everyone—the officers, inmates, and administration—was impacted by Mary's death. For the first time, we were one. United in our shared grief.

Town hall meetings were held in our individual units. There were tears and words of righteous indignation over the lack of medical care available to us. We were caught off guard by this sudden tragedy and loss, but it was how we responded that was important. Thankfully, most everyone responded in love, knowing God was in control. We prayed for Mary's family. We prayed for all the women in her unit, and we prayed to be able to find the good that would come from this tragedy.

I watched Mary's roommates return two bags of her bedding and clothing to the laundry. Others went through her personal belongings in her room and at her workplace. By evening, a memorial had been erected for her in the F3 multipurpose room at the table where she routinely played Skip-Bo, her favorite card game. Everyone signed a sympathy card that was mailed to her family.

Our Women of Warfare Conference, originally scheduled for that afternoon, was moved to the evening so that more inmates could attend. The visiting room was packed, and it was an awesome night of Spirit-filled worship. As we sang, I began to pray in my prayer language and told God I wanted to carry this story to the world.

Two days after Mary's passing, a memorial service was held in her honor. It was the first funeral I'd attended in prison. The skies opened up, and rain hit the ground. It appeared and felt as though tears were falling from heaven. I thought of Jeremiah 9:17–18: "Call for the mourners. Send for the women who mourn at funerals. Quick! Begin your weeping! Let the tears flow from your eyes." Given the somberness on the compound, I knew in my heart it was going to be a difficult evening.

Eventually, the rain stopped, and the sun peeked through the clouds. I waited to enter the memorial service until the procession of inmates from F3 ended. The inmates from Mary's unit entered hand in hand, two by two. Each wore their green uniform pants and either a white or gray T-shirt with a black ribbon pinned to it in honor of Mary. Ushers dressed in white escorted them to their seats.

F3 sat on the left side of the room, while inmates from the other three units were seated on the right. Palm leaves decorated both the front and back of the room, and "It Is Well with My Soul" played in the background as we entered. There was a picture of Mary, too, accompanied with the words, "Gone but not forgotten." A second sign contained Scripture from John 11:25: "I am the resurrection and the life." As I took my seat in the last row, I immediately felt God's presence.

The service began with a speech from the associate warden, who called Mary "a strong woman of God." He spoke about the impact people have on your life. Mary impacted many lives at Coleman, and it was obvious that her impact continued beyond her death. I learned that Mary was born in 1950, and prison had been her home for over sixteen years. She had received a twenty-five-year sentence and had seven years left to serve in prison after receiving a reduced sentence for good behavior.

Although I didn't know Mary well, she wore her emotions on her sleeve. She looked dejected every day when walking through the serving line. As sad as it was, I never saw her smile. Looking down at my prison boots, I wiped away a tear and wondered how many more people would endure what Mary did. My heart hurt, which told me the Holy Spirit was also grieving.

The service continued with praise and worship, and Mary's closest friends spoke about their relationships with "Miss Mary."

"We weren't just friends," one said. "We were family."

You have to be in prison to understand what that means. For some inmates, their fellow inmates are the only family they have ever truly known.

Another friend of Mary's, who was in her seventies, sang a song and received a standing ovation; one woman read a poem, and so many women shared funny stories. Mary was remembered as compassionate and kind, always wishing everyone a "good morning."

Mary was known for saying, "If you have a problem, get mad, cry, and get over it!" That sounded much too easy. Many women saw themselves in Mary, yet others saw Mary in their loved ones. Mary's best friend at Coleman, Miss Cook, could not even bring herself to attend the service.

Heartbroken, Wanda stepped up to the podium. Wanda was a member of my kitchen family. She was quiet, but she liked to make us laugh and was always joking around with the guards. She was also a hard worker and quick to lend a helping hand. Wanda stood in tears at the podium for close to a minute; it took everything she had to collect herself and muster the strength and courage to speak. I was about to encounter a side of Wanda that I had never met.

First, Wanda talked about how her own family had been impacted by prison. Many of her family members had been convicted on drug charges. Wanda's grandmother, for example, had received a twenty-four-year sentence and died in prison without Wanda having a chance to say goodbye. Her aunt received a thirty-three-year sentence, her cousin seventeen years, and her uncle received life in prison. Wanda sobbed uncontrollably as she said, "I have never told anyone the length of my sentence. I received sixteen and a half years." She kept crying and repeated over and over again, "We are good people. We are good people."

Wanda's speech left me in tears like most everyone else. Mary had been like a grandmother to Wanda, and her death brought up every painful emotion that Wanda had tried to suppress over the last seven years of her incarceration. In grieving Mary and sharing her pain, Wanda could finally let go of the shame and anger that she had held on to—over her charges, the length of her sentence, and the impact these crimes had on her family. Wanda had just touched hundreds of lives, including mine. I wiped away my tears, knowing God was once again working this situation for good and helping Wanda begin to heal her heart.

The next speaker was one of Mary's coworkers, who found a note in Mary's desk dated two years earlier. The word *repent* and the phrase "70 x 7" was written on the top of the page, followed by a list of verses that told us a little bit more about Mary's values and what she considered important:

Those who love their life in this world will lose it. Those who care nothing for their life in this world will keep it for eternity. Anyone who wants to serve me must follow me, because my servants must be where I am. And the Father will honor anyone who serves me. (John 12:25–26)

Only fools say in their hearts, "There is no God." They are corrupt, and their actions are evil; not one of them does good! The LORD looks down from heaven on the entire human race; he looks to see if anyone is truly wise, if anyone seeks God. But no, all have turned away; all have become corrupt. No one does good, not a single one! Will those who do evil never learn? (Psalm 14:1–4)

Mark chapter 7 was another passage that Mary loved. It teaches about inner purity, faith, and healing, and 2 Corinthians 5:21 was her signature verse and parting message to those she loved: "God made Christ, who never sinned, to be the offering for our sin, so that we could be made right with God through Christ."

Mary was a born-again Christian, and we all took comfort in knowing that Jesus ushered her into her heavenly home. What I did not realize was that given Mary's declining health, she had applied for a compassionate release and was awaiting a decision on her application. It was God, however, who ultimately set her free, and Mary would finally be reunited with her three children who predeceased her, two of whom, I was told, had died in prison.

I had another opportunity to minister to someone experiencing grief and loss while I was at Coleman. Crystal was in my unit and had already been in prison for six years on drug charges when I met her. She couldn't wait to return home and show everyone in her life the positive changes she had made. She was particularly excited for her ex-boyfriend, who was also the father of her daughter, to witness her transformation. They hadn't spoken in years, given his anger toward her and her incarceration, but she decided to step out in faith and call him. He answered, which Crystal considered a gift from God.

"I thought I was dreaming because all his anger was gone!" she told me. She ended up calling him a second time that evening and again the next day.

Crystal shared more with me about the situation with her ex-boyfriend, and she aired thoughts and feelings that she had clearly locked inside her heart for a long time. I shared Scripture with her on the importance of forgiving others and encouraged her to thank God for softening her ex's heart. We were thrilled about how things were working out between them, and it was obvious that Crystal's heart was experiencing major healing.

Just three days after our initial discussion, I was sitting outside and waiting to go to work when Crystal approached me with tears in her eyes.

"Katie," she started. "I need to tell you that my daughter's dad died...the ex-boyfriend that I told you about. I can't believe what God was able to do this week to make things right between us, and I just wanted to tell you that."

"I'm so sorry, Crystal," I told her. I went on to remind her that God is faithful and had bestowed a wonderful gift on the two of them by restoring their relationship.

In the days, weeks, and months that passed after the loss of her former boyfriend, Crystal remained a pillar of strength. She taught others about the gift of forgiveness and gave God the glory whenever she shared her miraculous testimony.

We all have a story. I have heard stories riddled with heartache and pain, others filled with violence and abuse, and still more of hopelessness and regret. God uses tough, painful experiences to conform us to his image and to win our hearts, and sometimes that tough, painful experience is death. God cares deeply every time that one of his loved ones dies, and he promises to work all things for good (Romans 8:28). Take Mary's death, for example. Her passing showed me how death can draw people together and facilitate healing. The death of Crystal's ex-boyfriend showed me that forgiveness is not only a choice but also a precious gift.

I can't say I ever thought I would have a prison ministry or start a foundation for children of incarcerated parents, but God placed those desires in my heart. He tells us in his Word, "Direct your children onto the right path, and when they are older, they will not leave it" (Proverbs 22:6). And Jesus said, "Let the children come to me. Don't stop them! For the Kingdom of Heaven belongs to those who are like these children" (Matthew 19:14).

More than 2.7 million children in the United States have an incarcerated parent, and half of these kids are under the age of ten. To put it another way, one out of every twenty-eight children has a mother or father in prison, and ten million children have experienced parental incarceration at some point in their lives.[14]

Every once in a while, I wondered how I would pull off my own ministry. I had no experience with nonprofit organizations or foundations, and I had never been involved with significant fundraising efforts. Furthermore, given my litigation expenses and the significant amount of restitution I still had to pay, I had absolutely no money to get this thing off the ground. But I knew that's where God would come in.

Thanksgiving and Christmas were around the corner, which reminded me to be thankful for everything God was doing in my life. Although no Christmas gifts awaited me, I discovered far better gifts in God's Word, gifts that remind us of God's love, goodness, grace, and mercy.

God saved you by his grace when you believed. And you can't take credit for this; it is a gift from God. (Ephesians 2:8)

The wages of sin is death, but the free gift of God is eternal life through Christ Jesus our Lord. (Romans 6:23)

God has given each of you a gift from his great variety of spiritual gifts. Use them well to serve one another. Do you have the gift of speaking? Then speak as though God himself were speaking through you. Do you have the gift of helping others? Do it with all the strength and energy that God supplies. Then everything you do will bring glory to God through Jesus Christ. All glory and power to him forever and ever! (1 Peter 4:10–11)

We celebrate the birth of Jesus on Christmas. Perhaps you wonder why Jesus came to earth in the first place. One reason is us—to save lost souls, to call us into repentance, and to testify the truth of God's Word. He also came to destroy evil and free people from the bondage of sin and the fear of death. His is the ultimate gift: the gift of forgiveness and everlasting life.

The highlight of my Christmas that year was spotting an eagle, which is a symbolic messenger of God. The eagle symbolizes swiftness and destruction. Eagles have great speed and often use the element of surprise, carrying off their prey before it can react. Why did I have a feeling a surprise was right around the corner?

Chapter 10

My surprise arrived in early January 2013, and it turned out to be a second written order of the court requesting my appearance to testify at the federal courthouse in Wisconsin.

I'd spoken with several inmates familiar with the transfer process ahead of time, and they told me the plane would first go to Oklahoma City, where the Federal Transit Center is located. Everyone must travel through the Federal Transit Center; it's like a distribution center for inmates. From there, inmates are transferred wherever they need to go to either serve their time or appear in court. That meant I'd likely fly from Tampa to Oklahoma City and then to Chicago for a vehicular transport to Milwaukee.

I sat in the cafeteria, waiting to be called to the receiving and discharge department to begin the transfer process and depart for Wisconsin. Carol sat next to me, and we reminisced about our time together at Coleman. The two of us somehow managed to complete a full year of Bible study and help other inmates draw closer to God. We learned a lot about ourselves and felt confident that countless ministry opportunities awaited us in the future.

Before parting, Carol and I tearfully prayed for divine protection. Then Carol walked away, saddened over my leaving, only to return a few minutes later with a message from above.

"Katie," she started, "I know how you feel about your case and the injustice you feel you've suffered, but God sent me back to tell you something important. These are the Lord's words, not mine: *This journey has never been about who was right or wrong; this journey has always been about your heart.* I broke down and cried, even though I knew all along that God only wanted the best for me.

A little before ten in the morning, an officer motioned for me to enter receiving and discharge. It was time to find the strength and courage inside myself to endure this transfer process again. I opened the door and saw the handcuffs, chains, and shackles waiting on the table. I paused, inhaled slowly, and then let out a long, deep breath.

The routine was familiar to me. If I had to use the restroom, now was the time to do that, so I did. Then a female officer escorted me into the dressing room, where I stripped down to my birthday suit, and then she searched my body in places where criminals are known to hide things. After the cavity search, I again put on my traveling clothes: a brown T-shirt, khaki-colored elastic waist pants, and blue slip-on tennis shoes.

I returned to the common area, where an officer secured my handcuffs, ankle cuffs, and waist chains. As he was securing my handcuffs, the warden walked in.

"What are the top three needs for children of incarcerated parents?" I asked her.

"These children need a liaison," she started. "Someone who can help them when their families aren't able to. Second, the kids need to visit their parents, but the cost of transportation is prohibitive."

She hesitated before telling me the children's third need. Instead, she asked me to identify the third need based on my personal experience at Coleman.

"Well, given close to 70 percent of the women at Coleman don't have a high school diploma, I believe inmates need an education. And to learn hands-on parenting skills for their children."

The warden nodded her head in agreement before leaving.

I wondered how many kids The Vivian Foundation would impact and how we would affect positive change for these families. The challenge ahead of me reminded me of David and Goliath. David was an Israelite and a lowly shepherd boy, whereas

Goliath was a Philistine and a nine-foot giant. The Israelites and the Philistines were at war, and twice a day for forty days, Goliath taunted the Israelites, daring them to send their own champion to fight him in single combat. Everyone in the Israelite army, including King Saul, were too scared—except David. David approached Goliath, who looked down at David and sneered, assuming it was all a joke. Most of us know the rest of the story from 1 Samuel 17, but for those who don't, David effortlessly conquered Goliath using only his sling and five smooth stones.

What was the key to David's success? It was his perspective. He assessed the situation from God's point of view. Whereas most of the Israelites looked at Goliath and only saw a fearsome giant, David saw a mortal man defying almighty God. And not only was Goliath too big of a target to miss, but David also knew he would not face the giant alone; God would fight with him.

I knew God would fight for The Vivian Foundation too. It was a kingdom project that would serve millions of children and their incarcerated parents. They were our (very big) target, our giant, so to speak. And like the lowly shepherd boy, The Vivian Foundation would rely on God to lead the way.

The white transport van waited outside, which meant it was time to venture into the unknown once again. The last time I'd left the facility, it was 95 degrees outside. On this day, however, the temperature was barely above 50 degrees. The skies were overcast, a light mist was falling, and the wind blew strong. It was cold by Florida's standards. Unfortunately, it does not matter how hot or cold it is outside; inmates must wear a short sleeve brown T-shirt, khaki-colored elastic waist pants, and blue slip-on tennis shoes.

Aside from the confinement, the most difficult part of the transfer process was dehydration. The Bureau of Prisons (BOP) provides a bag lunch but nothing to drink. No beverages mean fewer bathroom breaks, which makes the transfer process easier on the twelve US marshals assigned to the flight transporting over one hundred inmates. Most often, inmates are moved to attend court cases. In my instance, I was serving my time in Florida but needed to return to Milwaukee to testify before the court.

The ride from Coleman to Tampa was uneventful. We drove past the International Mall and onto airport property, and then memories from my first transfer process came rushing back. Both orderly and time-consuming, the process requires hundreds of inmates to move from a plane to transport vehicles and from transport vehicles to a plane. To me, it also felt heartless and inhumane. There I was, a nonviolent offender, and yet I was treated the same way as murderers, pedophiles, and terrorists.

I stepped onto the tarmac, where a dozen US marshals wearing bulletproof vests and carrying high-powered sharpshooting rifles surrounded us. Needless to say, I stood where I was told. Even though my entire body shivered from the brisk January wind, the marshals were in no hurry. They wore winter coats, hats, and gloves. We continued to stand on the tarmac for some time while the prisoners flying into Tampa moved from the plane to the transport vehicle.

Within a few minutes, a marshal carrying a clipboard called my name and used a black Sharpie marker to write an X on my left hand. The marshal informed me that the dreaded X meant I was heading to Grady County Jail in Chickasha, Oklahoma. There isn't enough space at the Federal Transit Center to hold all the transferring inmates, so the federal government contracts with jails and prisons across the country to house the overflow of inmates.

I had heard horror stories about Grady County Jail, also known as "Shady Grady." A Coleman inmate had even said to me before leaving, "Whatever happens, just hope you don't end up at Grady County."

Haven't I been through enough already? I thought. *Grady County makes my accommodations at Coleman seem like a luxury hotel.* Though futile, I hoped the light mist might wash away the X on my hand.

Finally ready to board the plane, I was searched a second time. A marshal hunting for contraband patted me down, peered inside my mouth and under my tongue, and asked me to remove my shoes. It required me to balance on one foot while lifting the other and simultaneously reach down to remove my shoes, all while my hands were cuffed and my ankles shackled. Not the easiest thing to do. In fact, it was so difficult that the marshal removed my shoes for me and put them back on.

Once the marshal finished searching me, I climbed the stairs and boarded the aircraft. The men were segregated from the women, who boarded first and sat toward the front of the plane. We were strictly instructed not to make conversation or eye contact with the male prisoners while they boarded. If we did not cooperate, they would remove our bathroom privilege.

I looked out the window, wishing I could go back in time and change things. I wiped away a tear, wondering how in the world I was going to survive this nightmare. Only one thing was certain: God had decided I would do this part of the journey alone. No phone, no email, and no one except the two of us.

The plane started its descent into Oklahoma City, and I dreaded what awaited me next. I had never been to the Sooner State, and a part of me hoped it would be my first and last trip. To my surprise, the Federal Transit Center was located on airport property, so we pulled right up to the facility. Most inmates on the flight were taken inside, but I was one of a handful of not-so-lucky ones to be transported to yet another location.

The Grady County Jail bus was ready and waiting. It looked like a normal school bus, except it was brown and white instead of yellow. Similar to the van that drove us to Tampa, the bus to Chickasha had metal barriers separating us from the two accompanying officers, one of whom drove. The other stood near the stairs, watching us and keeping his gun within our sight. We were like dogs locked inside a kennel.

Like the plane, the women were seated in front and the men in back and prohibited from interacting with each other. That didn't stop many of them from making sly, quiet comments anyway. I, on the other hand, kept my mouth shut.

Chickasha was approximately thirty-five miles southwest of Oklahoma City, yet the ride seemed to take forever. As we approached Grady County Jail late that afternoon, the bus pulled into a large indoor parking area. We were told to remain seated until the officers were in position and the garage door closed. Then we were allowed to exit the bus.

I stepped inside the building and stood with a group of other female prisoners also from the bus. One by one, an officer removed our restraints before ushering us into a holding cell. Of the ten of us who now occupied a relatively small space, six of us were "feds" (federal inmates) waiting for processing.

The motion sickness from the bus left me nauseous, and I had a splitting headache from exhaustion and dehydration. To add insult to injury, the body odor of the local inmates, who, according to one of them, had spent more than a week in this cell, tested my already queasy stomach. If that wasn't enough, one of the young girls in our cell was going through withdrawal from whatever drug she was addicted to and threw up, vomiting in the same toilet I had to use just a few minutes later. I passed on dinner that night.

We remained in the holding cell for close to three hours until each of us was booked. Then it was time for another mug shot. An officer weighed me, I answered a few questions, and then I was issued clothing: an orange pair of scrubs, two pairs of orange mesh underwear, and one pair of orange Crocs. When I returned from changing, an officer put the restraints back on. I waited on a bench until the other women completed the same process.

Once everyone was ready, the officers told us to follow them to an elevator. The door opened on the third floor, and an officer buzzed the command station. A thick steel door then opened, leading us to a small holding area. The heavy door closed behind us, and another door appeared, similar to the one we had just passed through.

Before walking through a third door, an officer removed my restraints, and I was handed a bag containing a one-inch-thick mat, a bloodstained sheet, a wool blanket with holes in it, half of a towel, and a few prison-issued toiletries. I had entered a real-life episode of *Lockdown*.

My home sweet home was now cell block (or pod) 3A–3, which was one of eight two-person rooms in the cell pod. I would share this six-by-eight-foot space with Trina, a county jail inmate who arrived a few months earlier. She had the lower bunk, which meant I was assigned the upper.

Like Coleman, the bunk was a thin metal tray that stood approximately five feet off the ground. I was not able to physically climb up there without stepping on the stainless-steel toilet and sink. I quickly realized it would be impossible for me to sleep on such a narrow surface. It was barely over two feet wide. I asked Trina if she minded if I slept on the concrete floor between her bed and the door instead. Thankfully, she didn't care.

I took a closer look at the door, which contained a small window and an even smaller opening for sliding through food trays. I started to feel claustrophobic.

"How long are we locked down?" I asked.

"Twelve hours a day," Trina answered.

"Do you mind if I leave the food tray door open?" I convinced myself that if the small door was open, I would breathe easier.

Within minutes of arriving in my cell, all the inmates were told to return to theirs for the evening. From eight in the evening till eight in the morning, we were in lockdown. The heavy door to our cell slammed shut and locked automatically. I was about to find out what it was like to sleep on the floor of a county jail cell.

I placed the paper-thin mat in the corner, hoping no insects or rodents would be joining me. I covered the mat with the bloodstained sheet and tried to make a pillow out of the tattered towel.

The ragged blanket would have to keep me warm, as I had not been given a T-shirt or socks. If there was ever a time that I needed my friends to pray for me, it was then. Unfortunately, they had no idea where I was.

I tried to make a collect call earlier that night to let my family know where I was. But most all the numbers I'd memorized were for cell phones, and people cannot accept collect calls on their mobile devices for security reasons. Some phone providers won't allow collect calls to be made to landlines either. After several futile attempts to reach someone, I gave up. I hoped caller ID would make my location known to someone, who would maybe let other friends and family know where I was.

I tossed and turned trying to get comfortable on the floor. Then I heard *bang, bang, bang, bang.* It was a continual clanging sound, like someone hitting a metal pipe with an aluminum baseball bat. I counted the repetition of the clanging. One, two, three, four...all the way up to thirty times before it stopped.

"What's that noise?" I asked Trina.

"That's the male inmate below who wants out," she explained. "He's been in solitary confinement for the last fifteen months."

"We're obviously not going to get much sleep," I conceded.

"We sleep when we can."

"How do you know he's been in solitary confinement for fifteen months?" I wondered out loud.

"He talks to some of the women through the air vents."

How can a person survive fifteen months of solitary confinement, where they're subjected to sensory deprivation and prohibited from any social contact? How can a person's mental health *not* be permanently impacted by such torment?

The pounding subsided, and I fell asleep for a short time, only to be awakened by a different noise.

"What's that?" I asked again. It sounded like chains dragging across the ground.

"Stand up and look out the window," Trina suggested. "Those are the men being moved."

"In the middle of the night?"

"Virtually every night. You'll get used to it," she assured me.

I wasn't sure I could ever get used to it. It all seemed so inhumane. As I lay in the dark on the cold floor, I realized I was not in a county jail; I was one step above hell. It was going to take everything I had to survive this part of the journey.

At four in the morning, the detention officers turned on the bright lights in our cells and unlocked our doors for breakfast. Since I hadn't eaten the day before, I figured I'd better see what was served.

Like our cell doors, the door separating our pod from the officers in the command center had a small opening through which they slid the meal trays. An inmate would then stack each tray on top of a metal picnic table bolted to the floor, and we ate in the common area.

The common area included four metal tables, each of which seated four. I chose to sit at the table nearest my cell and examine my food, which could only be described as some sort of slop. My tray also came with two pieces of white bread and a single serving of butter. Trina warned me that lunch wasn't served until early afternoon, so she encouraged me to eat something. I did the best I could.

I was not given a cup for a drink, so I borrowed one from Trina. To get a beverage with a meal, inmates had to slide a cup through our side of the door to an officer on the other side, who would fill it before passing it back to us. I ended up drinking some kind of fruit juice.

Those who ate breakfast did so in a hurry, as we only had about ten minutes before having to return to our cells for the remainder of lockdown. I watched Trina hurriedly gather bread and butter from people who didn't want theirs, and it dawned on me that I, too, should probably save extra food that might be edible in case I got hungry later.

Because I couldn't get in touch with anyone the night before, I couldn't order food (or anything else) from the commissary. A friend or family member has to order and purchase items for inmates online. Not only was I in a county jail, but I was also now an indigent inmate. My prison-issued toiletries were going to have to do, and I had no choice but to eat the food put in front of me, even though it was unidentifiable.

At eight o'clock that morning, the electronic lock on the cell door opened, and we could venture into the common area. There was a television, but most all the inmates were still asleep, so turning it on was not an option—unless I wanted to risk a fight, and I certainly didn't. I'd already been warned of an inmate who sometimes took out her anger on other inmates in our pod. (She was later moved to another pod after assaulting an inmate in ours.)

I wandered over to the pile of books next to the microwave and was happy to find two Bibles. I grabbed one, sat outside my cell, and started reading. For whatever reason, God led me to Scripture about redemption.

One of the first verses I read was Romans 3:24: "God, in his grace, freely makes us right in his sight. He did this through Christ Jesus when he freed us from the penalty for our sins." He then took me to Ephesians 1:7, and the theme of redemption continued: "He is so rich in kindness and grace that he purchased our freedom with the blood of his Son and forgave our sins." Then I turned to Isaiah: "Be just and fair to all. Do what is right and good, for I am coming soon to rescue you and to display my righteousness among you" (56:1). These verses to which the Lord had directed me emphasize his rescuing us from the bondage of sin. I knew he was speaking to me through his Word, so I knew it was time for me to write.

I found a couple of random pieces of paper and a pencil and returned to my cell. Sitting at a metal table and writing made me feel like the apostle Paul writing his letters to the church he dearly loved. Paul authored many letters that became books in the New Testament. He actually wrote four of them while he was imprisoned:

Ephesians, Philippians, Colossians, and Philemon. These four letters are among the most hopeful and encouraging in the Bible. They help us understand how we can find joy in our trials, peace in our suffering, and contentment in our circumstances.

Paul remained joyful throughout the years of his incarceration because he was able to see his circumstances from God's point of view. He focused on what he was supposed to do as a Christ-follower, not what he wanted to do. I imagine he wanted to quit, considering he was beaten, imprisoned, shipwrecked, and betrayed. But Paul had his priorities straight, and he was grateful for everything God had given him. He knew how to be content.

I continued to read for a while and jotted down a few notes. Since it was still fairly quiet in the pod, I was lucky enough to fall back asleep until lunch time arrived at 12:30.

One by one, the inmates emerged from their cells and into the common area, rubbing their eyes and stretching. It was my first time seeing them since I'd arrived at night and since most of them chose not to eat breakfast.

I sat at a table with Trina and two women named Donna and Sasha. Everyone was subdued while eating. Inmates don't usually discuss the reason for their incarceration, yet these three ladies started to share their stories with me. Just like at Coleman, these women's problems included illegal drug possession and manufacturing, substance abuse, theft, and child neglect. My heart ached as they told me their children's names and ages and how their incarceration was impacting their families.

At two o'clock, I found myself back in my cell. Sasha sat next to me at the small table near the cell door, and Trina and Donna sat on Trina's bottom bunk. I knew in my heart this was a divine appointment, so I shared my testimony, my love for the Lord, and how he was working in my life. I told them about The Vivian Foundation and the book I was writing.

They were curious to know more about how God speaks to me and what it means to follow God's will. The Holy Spirit guided my words when I started to tell them how I'd been spending hours a day in prayer since the beginning of my incarceration. I explained that when we pray in our spiritual language, we develop an incredible connection with the Holy Spirit. I went on to tell them I had done everything God had asked of me, all of which continued to be instrumental to my spiritual growth and healing.

At that point in our conversation, I opened up about something I had never told anyone. I had a feeling I was sexually abused as a child, and I'd been racking my brain trying to remember if anything like this happened. In fact, I have happy memories of my childhood.

I shared with the ladies that during the second week of October, while at Coleman, I had the worst nightmare of my life. In this dream, I was young, about three or four years old, and wearing a white dress. I saw myself standing alone and crying as I kept repeating, *Stop it! It hurts! Stop it!* It was unnerving and upsetting to see myself at such an innocent age and hear my cries of despair.

When I woke up, I told the Lord, *I rebuke that dream in the name of Jesus. The devil must flee!* But then I quickly added, *God, I never want to experience anything like that again. But if this revelation came from you and is meant to help my heart heal, then bring it on.*

Less than a week after my nightmare, I was walking along the track at Coleman and praying when a name popped into my head and stopped me dead in my tracks. It was a name I was familiar with, a nickname. In that moment, God revealed to me my abuser. It was a man who lived in our neighborhood.

After sharing these details with Sasha, Donna, and Trina, I told them about the message Dale had received about me from God. He had told her there was something deep inside my heart that I needed to give him—something no one else knew—before I could finally have peace. Sasha, Donna, and Trina were captivated by my story as I recalled other encounters with Dale and how God so often used her to speak to me.

Step Into Prison, Step Out in Faith

I told the ladies how Dale kept telling me that God was going to send me a special child. This child would be a girl and a spitfire who "had a lot of Katie in her." I shared that the Lord said it would take everything in me to help this girl recover from her pain but that I would be successful in supporting her on her journey.

Trina was beginning to shake, so I paused. She covered her mouth with her hands, and tears welled in her eyes. Sasha looked at me in disbelief, and Donna put her arm around Trina. Struggling to get the words out, a wide-eyed Donna said, "Katie, Trina is that special child."

In awe and unable to speak, I realized what was happening. Everything started to make sense. God had revealed a number of times to me that there would be a miracle of forgiveness.

Donna and Sasha continued, telling me they had been trying for months to help Trina cope with the pain of the childhood sexual abuse she'd suffered at the hands of her father. For the next three hours, Trina poured her heart out to me, sharing horrific graphic details. The abuse started when she was nine years old and continued until she was fourteen. Trina was certain her mother knew what was going on, and yet her mother did nothing to stop it.

We talked at great length about Trina's parents, her siblings, her children, and her struggles. Trina continued to cry, and I continued to encourage her. I leveraged every Bible verse on forgiveness that I could in hopes of helping her heart begin to heal.

"Trina," I started, "the best gift you can give yourself and your parents is the gift of forgiveness. It is a gift found deep within your heart, and it's a gift filled with love. Forgiveness is also a choice. It doesn't mean what your mom and dad did was right; it was very, very wrong. You were deeply hurt for years. Now leave it in God's hands so that you can be at peace. He will take care of it." I paused for a minute before adding, "God tells us to pray for those who have hurt us."

So we prayed. And prayed. And prayed. Then Trina decided to make a godly decision. She chose to forgive her mother and father.

The burden and emotional distress she had been carrying for thirty years had finally been lifted. We had just experienced a miracle.

Later that evening, physically and emotionally drained, I sat in the dark on the floor of my cell, thinking about the day's events. I couldn't believe how God had accomplished this, considering everything that had to happen for Trina and me to end up in the same jail cell at the same time.

With my back propped up against the wall and my hands resting on bent knees, I thanked God for this miracle. I was so overcome by the presence of the Holy Spirit that I could hardly believe everything that had transpired. Through tears, I spoke the following words out loud: "God has just climbed the fire escape with my bouquet of roses." God, my Prince Charming, had arrived to fill my heart with his love. I felt like his princess.

My coming to Grady County Jail was unquestionably orchestrated from above. This was my time to grieve the innocence I lost as a young child. I, too, had a choice to make, and like Trina, I made the godly decision to forgive my abuser.

God gently reminded me that no one knew about the abuse I suffered and that my family should have been able to trust this man. Even though he had passed away many years ago, the thought of him having potentially hurt other children in our neighborhood, possibly members of my very own family, was painful and disturbing. But I found comfort in his Word: "If you cause one of these little ones who trusts in me to fall into sin, it would be better for you to be thrown into the sea with a large millstone hung around your neck" (Mark 9:42).

Victims of childhood sexual abuse do not always remember their experiences and, as a result, do not know or understand why they feel like something's wrong with them as people. For most of my life, I wondered why I behaved the way I did. Why did I always feel such great shame, embarrassment, and confusion about sex? Why was sex always so difficult for me to talk about? Was my discomfort why I always found it necessary to joke about sexual intimacy or make inappropriate comments? Was the abuse I suffered the reason why I never felt loved and why I struggled to articulate my love for others? I should have been able to find love and intimacy in my marriage, yet it escaped me.

While pondering these questions, I felt relief wash over me. There was nothing wrong with me because of anything I had done; it was what had been done to me. Whereas most children learn to set boundaries (of sorts) at an early age, my abuser had ignored my boundaries, disrespected them and me. And when it came time to set boundaries as a teenager and as an adult, I either could not or would not because I was paralyzed with fear.

As long and difficult as my journey had been thus far, every bit of it was necessary to release me from my painful past and the bondage of sin. Who would have ever thought God would do his best work in a county jail cell in Chickasha, Oklahoma? After years and years of searching, I had finally found true love in the Lord.

Chapter 11

On Sunday morning, I woke up in Grady County Jail, questioning whether I had the physical and mental fortitude to survive this place. I seemed to be the only one trying to maintain somewhat of a normal schedule, although nothing about life in jail is normal. Then I learned that Mondays and Thursdays were transport days to Chicago, and with any luck, I would be out of Shady Grady first thing in the morning.

I'd slept for an hour or two before an officer's voice spoke through the two-way intercom in the cell, waking me up around 2:00 a.m. on Monday morning.

"Scheller?" the voiced asked.

"Yes?" I answered. Each cell had a microphone.

"You're leaving today. Get ready."

I did not go back to sleep and instead stared out the window, which overlooked a brick wall. My traveling clothes eventually arrived, and thankfully, it didn't take long for the officer to unlock the door. I couldn't wait to change out of the orange clothes I'd been wearing since Friday and into the beige traveling clothes. Now that I was familiar with the transfer process, I knew I had better eat something, so I ate half of the stale bologna sandwich in the bagged lunch given to me for breakfast. I also knew to drink very little since I didn't know when I would be permitted to use a toilet again.

At about four in the morning, two officers arrived to chain and shackle me. Now I was one of the inmates whose chains and shackles dragging across the ground would wake the others. I was then led back down to the first floor and sat on a bench for what seemed to be close to an hour before boarding the bus. It was still dark outside when we pulled out of the garage. We first drove to another building that housed inmates, and a few prisoners climbed aboard. It was time to head back to the airport in Oklahoma City.

Once we arrived at the airport, the plane was already out of the hangar and waiting on the tarmac. We sat inside the bus for quite some time while the driver studied his clipboard. The other inmates were allowed to exit the vehicle as the transfer process began, but I was asked to remain seated.

One of the officers was talking about me to someone on his cell phone, and then he turned around and asked if I had been tested for tuberculosis. I told him I had not been tested while I was at Grady County Jail, but I had been tested within the last year at Coleman. Each prisoner is required to be screened for tuberculosis before being transported, but I hadn't been at Grady long enough to have had the test performed.

His phone conversation continued, and he noted something in the paperwork on his clipboard. The deputy then told me I could exit the bus and get in line for a pat down. Part of me didn't want to venture outside because it was so cold, but I decided I was ready for whatever awaited me in Chicago. My accommodations there could not possibly be worse than Shady Grady's.

With the pat down complete, I climbed the stairs to board the airplane and chose an aisle seat near the front. I was exhausted from having slept so little. A US marshal boarded soon after I did.

"Scheller?" the marshal called.

Uh-oh, I thought, before letting him know I was the person he had just called.

"Get off the plane," he said. "They don't want you." By *they*, he meant the federal prosecutors in my case, more specifically the US Attorney for the Eastern District Court in Wisconsin.

You have got to be kidding me, my thoughts reeled. *Not again!*

"Now what?" I asked the marshal.

"You're going back to Grady County. Get on the bus."

What in the world was happening? I could not believe what I had just been told. Did the last defendant in my case accept a plea deal, or was the case delayed again?

The US marshal said I would probably be transferred back to Coleman eventually, but he had no idea when.

I climbed onto the bus and saw the two male officers from Grady but no one else. I was chained and shackled and all alone with them. I felt a knot in my stomach. Not all prison guards can be trusted, and sexual abuse is not uncommon. As a matter of fact, a lawsuit against the guards at Coleman was eventually filed, and many of the male guards were fired and later charged.

Much to my surprise, the two gentlemen were extremely nice and wanted to know what I did to end up in federal prison.

I laughed. "You wouldn't believe me if I told you."

Since the bus couldn't leave Oklahoma City until the plane was airborne, I shared my story with them while we waited. The three of us had an enjoyable conversation on the ride back.

Once we arrived in Chickasha, the two officers escorted me inside, and I told both deputies I needed to use the restroom. Neither acknowledged my request. One of the officers removed my chains and shackles before apologizing for having to put me in the holding cell that stood before me. I didn't see a toilet in the cell, so I reminded him that I needed to use the restroom. He pointed at the drain in the floor and then locked the door.

The cell was extremely small, like that of a small walk-in closet, and no bigger than seventy square feet. It lacked a window, and I felt the concrete walls closing in on me. I desperately needed to relieve myself and dared to peek inside the drain. I saw feces and a bloody sanitary napkin and quickly looked away, gagging from both the sight and the smell. But I also had no choice; I had to go. Reluctantly, I squatted over the drain as if I were on some horrific camping trip.

Step Into Prison, Step Out in Faith

I feared how long I might be kept in this filthy torture chamber. On the Friday night I first arrived at Grady, we were kept in the larger holding cell for three hours. Now, with nowhere to sit except the unsanitary floor, I remained standing. And there was only one thing I could do. I stood in the corner, facing the camera, and began to pray in tongues. It was just the Holy Spirit and me, and I prayed until that door finally opened over an hour later.

Next, I was taken into the booking area and again issued a pair of orange scrubs, orange Crocs, and two pairs of mesh underwear. Chained and shackled again, I was led upstairs to return to cell block 3A–3. The inmates were surprised to see me, and I was equally surprised to find a relatively clean sheet and a newer blanket in my bedding bag. I was so exhausted that I felt sick and had a splitting headache. I had never felt so physically and emotionally sapped in my life. I set up my bed on the floor and slept until dinner.

My family still didn't know where I was, so I wrote a letter to my sister. The mail would not go out until the next day, but if I were lucky, she would receive my letter before the end of the week and place a commissary order for me. The first item on my list was a travel-size pillow, and I also asked for toiletries and edible—although not exactly healthy—food: chips, candy, and cookies. Canned vegetables were the norm, and an occasional apple or banana would find its way onto the meal tray, although the fruit was usually borderline rotten or, on the other side of the spectrum, unripe. It's nearly impossible to peel an unripe orange.

After dinner I paged through one of the Bibles on the bookshelf in the pod and noticed someone had already circled some verses.

The LORD said to me, "Write my answer plainly on tablets, so that a runner can carry the correct message to others. This vision is for a future time. It describes the end, and it will be fulfilled. If it seems slow in coming, wait patiently, for it will surely take place. It will not be delayed." (Habakkuk 2:2–3)

God had encouraged me with this Scripture before. In this chapter of Habakkuk, evil and injustice appear to have an upper hand in the world. Habakkuk complained to God about it, and God's answer to him was the same as it would be to us—to wait patiently. Again, God was reminding me to be patient.

On Thursday, I finally connected with the outside world when the Holy Spirit led me to call my friend Marsha, who was one of the few people I could always count on. When Marsha accepted the collect call, I was so relieved to hear a familiar voice that I almost started crying. Marsha had been in contact with my family and told me that the last defendant had accepted a plea deal, which meant I wouldn't have to testify. And it turned out that the written order of the court had been canceled on the same day I was transferred out of Coleman and into Shady Grady, but word of the cancellation didn't reach Coleman in time.

Not having to testify was great news and an answered prayer. I would still be eligible for a downward departure for having cooperated, and it was exactly what God told me would happen. When Shawn, my friend from Coleman, received her downward departure, I had heard the Holy Spirit tell me that I, too, would receive one.

While lying on the floor of my cell and pondering everything that happened, I heard the Spirit begin to speak to me. Earlier, God had led me to the book of Joshua and the story of Jericho. In it, God chose Joshua, a man of great faith and exceptional leadership, to lead the Israelites into the promised land after Moses died.

God said to Joshua, "Be strong and courageous, for you are the one who will lead these people to possess all the land I swore to their ancestors I would give them...Be careful to obey all the instructions Moses gave you. Do not deviate from them, turning either to the right or to the left. Then you will be successful in everything you do" (Joshua 1:6–7). God continued, "Do not be afraid or discouraged. For the LORD your God is with you wherever you go" (v. 9).

Step Into Prison, Step Out in Faith

Because the people of Jericho feared the Israelites, the gates to their town were tightly shut when Joshua and the Israelites arrived. No one inside the walls was allowed to go in or out. The Lord then instructed Joshua to lead the Israelites in marching around the walls of Jericho once a day for six days and then seven times on the seventh day.

Joshua and the Israelites followed the Lord's command, and on the seventh day, the Israelites woke at dawn and continued to march around the town. On their seventh lap, Joshua commanded the people, "Shout! For the LORD has given you the town!" (6:15–16). The walls of Jericho miraculously came tumbling down, and the Israelites charged into the city. Because Joshua listened and moved just as God instructed him, the Israelites successfully captured Jericho.

For months, we at Coleman had been hearing rumors that the federal government would no longer fund prison camps. We prayed for the walls of Coleman to tumble down like the walls of Jericho, releasing us to home confinement instead of the confines of prison. Obviously, that didn't happen, but something Trina, my cellmate at Grady, had said about walls kept rising up in my spirit. She said she had finally removed the wall surrounding her heart.

In a moment of divine revelation, I realized that I, too, had a wall surrounding my heart. I didn't want to experience any more hurt, so I built a wall to protect myself from others. But once I recognized its presence and understood how it impacted my behavior, the wall instantly came tumbling down. That was why I had to go to Grady—to stop beating myself up over my poor decisions and my subsequent behavior, both of which led to my incarceration.

The Lord helped me understand that the abuse was the reason why I hadn't been able to exhibit true godly love. It was also the reason I hadn't understood or dealt with my fear of being alone. For the first time in my life, I understood why I behaved the way I did. This revelation allowed me to finally give God everything he asked of me. In return, he showed me his love, kindness, and faithfulness by granting me peace. All the stress I put on myself for everything that had happened and for the people I had hurt vanished.

Soon after my divine realization, I was watching the Green Bay Packers football game on Saturday night and visiting with a new inmate. She was quiet and reserved but opened up to me. I learned that she was only twenty-three years old, although she looked younger than her age. She was also very pregnant and back in prison for having violated her probation.

I shared my testimony with her, and we talked about the meaning of being born again. I wanted to build trust with her while she reflected on her life decisions and their consequences, which she admitted weren't exactly great. Sunday morning, the Lord woke me up and told me it was time to invite her to the best party in town. While sharing an orange, I led her in prayer, and she accepted Jesus into her life as her Lord and Savior. Again, I was right where I was supposed to be, where God wanted me.

Monday was a day of reflection. I realized that before my incarceration, I had never had to wear the same clothes for over a week. I never had to sleep on a concrete floor—with stained sheets and ratty, threadbare blankets, no less. My diet was never limited to unappetizing food. I never had to use the bathroom in front of others, and I never lived in fear of the people around me, many of whom suffered from mental illness and addiction. Then it hit me. Plenty of people, too many people, live like that every day. Most of them probably aren't even in prison.

We all experience our own type of personal prison, our own unique struggles. It could be drugs, alcohol, trauma, mental health, loneliness, anger, bitterness, resentment, or a combination of those things. The world itself is rife with struggles, pain, and heartache. Reports of war, mass shootings, corruption, gang-related violence, sex trafficking, and racism, among countless other crises, routinely dominate headline news.

Like Habakkuk, we can either complain about evil and injustice or wait patiently for God to give us an opportunity to do something about it. I got face down on the floor of my cell and prayed in the Spirit, thanking God for my experience inside Shady Grady. I needed to witness and experience this side of life firsthand. I needed to understand the challenges inmates and their families face.

Just before we were locked down for the evening, a guard told me I would return to Coleman the next day. I felt like I'd won the lottery! But it also meant I had to say goodbye to Trina, the special child God had sent to me. In some ways, I felt guilty for leaving. Poor Trina had been charged with theft but was not yet convicted. But because she couldn't make bail, she had been stuck in Grady, away from her three children for months, and without a court date within sight.

I reconciled my conflicting feelings by reminding myself I had done all that God asked of me. Both Trina and I received the miracle of forgiveness; we forgave our abusers and ourselves. Still, it didn't make saying goodbye any easier. When it came time to leave, we embraced, and she thanked me for everything I had done to help her. She also gave me her home address so that I could keep in touch (and I have). I hoped and prayed she would be released for time served once she went before a judge (and that's what happened).

It's difficult to explain the bond you form with certain inmates, even after knowing them for just a short time. I guess that's because we are all children in God's family. As much as I was ready to leave Chickasaw and return to Florida, I could not help but think about the day ahead for all the inmates. They faced challenges every single day that I suspect many people, if not most, would not be able to survive.

I changed out of my Grady County scrubs and into my traveling clothes, dreading another eight hours in shackles and chains. I was also grateful for this part of my journey to come to an end. Psalm 91 came to mind: "The LORD says, 'I will rescue those who love me. I will protect those who trust in my name. When they call on me, I will answer; I will be with them in trouble. I will rescue and honor them'" (vv. 14–15).

In Oklahoma City, I boarded the plane bound for Tampa. I sat in an aisle seat. The female inmate seated by the window turned to me and asked, "What in the world are you doing here? You don't look like you would even jaywalk."

"I wouldn't!" I laughed. "As a matter of fact, I once wrote a check for fifty cents and mailed it to the State of Illinois after missing a toll."

The US marshal near us laughed too. "I agree," he said. "You don't look like you belong here. What did you do?"

"It's a long story," I responded. "And some day you can read all about it in the book I'm writing."

Touching down on the runway in Tampa brought a smile to my face. And once I was back at Coleman and fully processed, I walked into the compound and found my friends waiting for me. It turned out that they knew about my transfer back to the Sunshine State long before I did. And as strange as it sounds, it was great to be back.

Upon my return, one woman commented, "I don't know what God did to you, but you look different! You have a sparkle in your eyes that's been missing!"

I knew why my sparkle returned. It was because my experience at Grady had reinvigorated me on my mission to help inmates connect and grow in their relationship with God. I made a point to meet with our chaplain to discuss getting the "Just One Word" calendars into the hands of the women at Coleman. Again, the calendars feature a Bible reading plan to encourage people to spend time in God's Word each day.

I met with Chaplain Bass to discuss the calendars for 2013. A few days later, I met with the supervisory chaplain overseeing the compound. Both chaplains were on board with the plan, and our goal was to get the calendar into all five facilities at Coleman.

However, I was overwhelmed with frustration over the next few weeks. It started when I expressed to Chaplain Bass that I was disappointed by how long it was taking to get the calendars into the camp. My friend Ruth Ann Nylen, founder of Really Good News Ministries, which produced and shipped the calendars, received confirmation that they arrived at the complex, so I knew they were somewhere on the grounds. Yet there seemed to be no sense of urgency in locating and distributing them.

Chaplain Bass insisted the devil caused my aggravation and that I needed to rebuke it. I, however, wasn't convinced that my frustration was the devil's work. I was simply being impatient. My passion for providing desperately needed spiritual resources to the inmates at Coleman fueled my frustration. Nevertheless, the matter wasn't worth debating with the chaplain.

Sometimes God, not the Enemy, places discontentment in our spirit. In his book, *Source of My Strength*, Dr. Charles Stanley teaches that a restless feeling deep inside our soul can be one of the most exciting times in our life. It's a sign that God is at work and preparing to promote us to a deeper, more fulfilling role.[15] The good news is that once we step onto God's new path for us and embrace his guidance, the discontent and frustration disappear.

On Sunday, February 24, 2013, I arrived at church a few minutes early to find well over one hundred women holding their calendars. Chaplain Bass spoke about them and gave a shout-out to Ruth Ann. The chaplain went on to share that I had a hand in their development and called me to the front of the chapel to acknowledge my ministry work. The inmates gave me a standing ovation, and the chaplain handed me the microphone.

Before speaking, I kissed my fingers and pointed to heaven. I went on to explain to the crowd the structure of the Bible reading plan and how to use it. And I promised the women that if they provided me the names and addresses of their children and grandchildren, the ministry would see to it that their families received the kids' version of the calendar. The last thing I shared was God having revealed to me that I would become involved in a prison ministry.

"God told me to set up a nonprofit organization called The Vivian Foundation," I said. "It will help families impacted by incarceration, especially children."

As I took my seat, Chaplain Bass spoke about my tenacity and passion in getting the calendars into all five of the facilities at Coleman, including the penitentiaries.

"Have you ever thought you could do something to bless seven thousand inmates?" Chaplain Bass asked the crowd. "This girl is not playing. She's serious about what she's doing."

She then introduced our guest speaker, Chaplain Rock, and little did I know that he would use me as an example throughout his sermon. He started out with a story from Matthew 8:1–4.

> Large crowds followed Jesus as he came down the mountainside. Suddenly, a man with leprosy approached him and knelt before him. "Lord," the man said, "if you are willing, you can heal me and make me clean." Jesus reached out and touched him…"Don't tell anyone about this. Instead, go to the priest and let him examine you. Take along the offering required in the Law of Moses for those who have been healed of leprosy. This will be a public testimony that you have been cleansed."

I interpreted Chaplain Rock's use of this story as a challenge he was presenting to us: Did we truly believe God could heal us and use us for his kingdom? The story also taught us a lesson—to show our faith, not just tell of it. I personally had been sensing God reminding me to do as I was told and to trust that my actions and testimony would speak for themselves.

Chaplain Rock then referenced Isaiah 61:1, which reads, "The Spirit of the Sovereign LORD is upon me, for the LORD has anointed me to bring good news to the poor. He has sent me to comfort the brokenhearted and to proclaim that captives will be released and prisoners will be freed." This verse encourages us that we can bring good news to those who need to hear of Jesus.

Chaplain Rock continued, "There's a prisoner who has already been set free. Can you believe what God is doing with an inmate who has nothing? That is divine favor! Thousands of calendars? God is blessing others and will bless Scheller for her obedience."

He went on to encourage us to become everything we could be and asked if we were persistent enough to get what we wanted. "You have to get up and be willing to do whatever he's asking you to do," he said. "God has given Scheller a vision."

Chaplain Rock then looked directly at me. "This is the beginning," he said. "May he bless you in all that you do." I was so overcome by God's presence that all I could do was rest my head in my hands and weep.

"Scheller didn't brag about what she had done; she waited until the chaplain called her up so that God would get the glory," Chaplain Rock pointed out. "This sister found a way to get the calendars done, and in the process, she's become a woman of elegance. It's what's on the inside, ladies. It comes from the heart. Let others see the power and the glory of God in your deliverance. You must be an extension of God's love."

A month later, something quite interesting happened. I had finished reading a book, so I headed to the library to check out a new one, and *A Love Worth Giving* by Max Lucado found its way into my hands. I returned to my cell and read through chapter five by eight thirty that night, when my eyes started to grow heavy. I decided to take a quick nap before ten o'clock count, but I kept tossing and turning like a fish out of water.

Frustrated, I asked the Lord, *What are you trying to tell me?*

Read your book and you will have your answer, came his reply.

I grabbed the book and picked up where I left off. One page later, I found my answer in one of Max's stories. He had missed a flight because of a snowstorm in the Midwest. A stewardess told him all the coach seats on the next flight were full, so the airline needed to bump him up to first class. Max then writes that he boarded the plane and was so happy with his upgrade that he "smiled like a prisoner on early parole!"[16]

These kinds of surprises from the Lord are always exciting. I knew without a doubt that God led me to this story to assure me that I would receive early parole. And the chapter ended on this note: "So loosen up and enjoy the journey. You are going home in style."[17]

On May 9, 2013, the criminal case with my former employer finally ended. The last defendant had been sentenced to six months in prison, six months of home confinement, and two years of supervised release. With the case now closed, my attorney could file the motion for my downward departure. Within a few weeks of filing, my lawyer received notice that the federal US attorney was recommending a five-month reduction in my thirty-six-month sentence.

The next step in the downward departure process was a hearing during which the US attorney and my attorney would present their arguments to Judge Clevert, who would then ultimately decide how much time to reduce from my sentence. My spiritual support team and I prayed and believed I would be granted an immediate release.

The hearing took place on July 17 as a phone conference in my counselor's office. Once introductions were made, the US attorney spoke first and shared his recommendation for the five-month downward departure. My attorney reminded the court of everything I endured, having been transferred not once but twice and spending twelve days in Grady County Jail. I was then allowed to read the statement I'd prepared, which included my work in developing the content for both the children's and adult's "Just One Word" calendars and distributing seven thousand copies at Coleman.

Judge Clevert asked the US attorney whether he had considered the fact that I was transported twice, and the attorney said he had. My attorney and I were not so sure, and apparently, the judge agreed with us because he reduced my sentence by eight months without hesitation. The phone call came to an abrupt end, and I sat in stunned silence, not knowing what to think.

Every major event or milestone in the legal process stirs everything up all over again—the thoughts, emotions, fears, and regrets. I brooded over my poor decisions. I relived the day I pled guilty and how I returned to Tampa a total wreck. I revisited my sentencing date, replaying in my head the sound of Judge Clevert's direct, stern tone as he rendered the verdict. I remembered the weight of the cold chains and shackles so well I could still feel them on my wrists and ankles. Hadn't I been through enough?

I had been hoping and praying to walk out of Coleman that day, but as God's Word tells us, "You can make many plans, but the LORD's purpose will prevail" (Proverbs 19:21). In many ways, I was surprised I wasn't granted an immediate release. Between the eight-month sentence reduction and the reduction for my good behavior, I should have already been in a halfway house. I'd had enough, and I wondered why other people who did the same thing that I did went unpunished. I just wanted it to be over.

Then I remembered this experience was part of my divine destiny. Hebrews 10:32–36 resonated deeply within me:

> Think back on those early days when you first learned about Christ. Remember how you remained faithful even though it meant terrible suffering. Sometimes you were exposed to public ridicule and were beaten, and sometimes you helped others who were suffering the same things. You suffered along with those who were thrown into jail, and when all you owned was taken from you, you accepted it with joy. You knew there were better things waiting for you that will last forever. So do not throw away this confident trust in the Lord. Remember the great reward it brings you! Patient endurance is what you need now, so that you will continue to do God's will. Then you will receive all that he has promised.

It took a few weeks for the computer system to reflect my new release date: January 13, 2014. On that day, I would be released from the Bureau of Prison's custody and begin my one year of probation at home in Wisconsin. I now faced a decision as to what to do between now and then. Should I go to a halfway house in Milwaukee or serve the remainder of my sentence at Coleman?

If I wanted to stay at Coleman, I'd have to petition the administrative team for an exemption from the halfway house. I knew which way I was leaning, but it was not my decision. I'd been asking God what I should do and where I should go in order to stay in his perfect will for my life.

My answer arrived not long after the downward departure hearing. I was sitting on my bed when my case manager, Miss Adams, walked past the door to my cell and stopped.

"Aren't you supposed to be in 404?" she asked.

"No," I answered. "I've been in 401 for quite some time."

Miss Adams said, "The computer says you're in 404. You better go see your counselor and make sure." Then she handed me a note that had my new release date printed on it.

I went to see my counselor, and she pulled up my inmate number.

"It says 401. See?" she said, showing me her computer screen.

Once again, I knew this incident was a message from God. I would find the answer to my probation location in 404. Jeremiah 40:4 reads, "I am going to take off your chains and let you go. If you want to come with me to Babylon, you are welcome. I will see that you are well cared for. But if you don't want to come, you may stay here. The whole land is before you—go wherever you like."

God said I could go wherever I liked, and I had no desire to move to a halfway house. They aren't usually in the best neighborhoods, and I knew the halfway house in Milwaukee was no exception. Some houses are also coed, which makes for other challenges. Other inmates who'd been released to halfway houses all said the same thing: "If I knew how bad it was going to be, I would have stayed in prison."

I decided to complete my prison sentence at Coleman, which proved a wise decision, given that there were several shootings in the area near the halfway house in Milwaukee the very week that I made up my mind. I must be among the very few people who have chosen to stay in prison once given the opportunity to leave.

On one of my Sundays off from my job in the kitchen, I crawled back into bed for an afternoon nap. In my dream, I had to go to the Milwaukee airport to pick up my son, whose flight was expected to arrive at 2:13 p.m. When I woke up, I started looking through my Bible. Only one 2:13 verse spoke to my heart: "God is working in you, giving you the desire and the power to do what pleases him" (Philippians). I had been asking God why I was still in prison and what he wanted me to do or learn, and this verse was my answer. He was still working in me and giving me the power to fulfill his will for my life.

That same day, I was in the library searching for another new book to read since I'd finished Max Lucado's. Before I could find one, the horn to return to our units for four o'clock count went off, so I returned to my unit empty-handed. After dinner, though, I went back to the library and found *God's Power to Change Your Life* by Rick Warren. I checked it out and read the first 125 pages in one evening.

The following night, the weather was beautiful, so I grabbed the book and headed outside to read some more. After reading for a bit longer, I smiled. Here is what I found.

> God did not save us because of our goodness but because of his own kindness and mercy. Thanks to the saving work of Jesus Christ our Savior, God can declare us good. Our goodness is a gift from God. We cannot work for it. We cannot earn it. We do not deserve it.

The Bible calls this work of Christ *justification*. That is a big word that simply means God says you are okay because of what Jesus did for you. When you put your trust in Christ, God gives you a new nature. (It's like starting over; that is why it is called being "born again"). Then God not only gives you the desire to do good, but also gives you the power to do good. Philippians 2:13 says, "It is God who works in you both to will and to do His good pleasure" (NKJV). He gives you the desire and the power to do what is right.[18]

I walked over to one of my friends sitting at a nearby picnic table. "What numbers did I tell you about this afternoon?" I asked.

"Two thirteen," she said. Then I showed her what I had just read, and a look of shock appeared on her face.

I headed back upstairs to jot down some notes, and while I was sitting on my bed, God told me to jump ahead to page 213. This page mentioned the same verse and echoed a similar message from the passage I read earlier: "Philippians 2:13 says, 'For God is at work within you, helping you want to obey him, and then helping you do what he wants.' God not only gives you the desire to do right, but also gives you the power to do what is right."[19] I thought I was going to have a heart attack! I picked up the book and headed back outside.

"What now?" asked the group of ladies, now curious, sitting around the picnic table. They often asked me what the numbers of the day were.

"You guys are not going to believe what just happened." I shared my latest encounter and my testimony with the ladies, who remained open and receptive to what I had to say in sharing God's Word with them.

Still, my mind reeled. How did God compel me to go back to the library a second time that day? How did God ensure I would choose to read Warren's book, which was not on the shelves when I was browsing earlier that afternoon, and yet it was there at six in the evening? How did I dream about a 2:13 landing time? How did he place all those ladies together at the picnic table to hear his Word? How did Rick Warren's book happen to have Philippians 2:13 on page 213? And how did I hear God tell me to turn to that page in the first place?

In the Bible, God uses all kinds of different methods to communicate with his people: dreams, visions, angels, prophetic voices, and the teachings of his Son, Jesus. Sometimes God's methods for reaching us are surprising; he once even used a talking donkey (Numbers 22:28)! He speaks to our hearts, and he wants us to hear him. The absolute best way to hear God's voice is to read his written Word. It details his will for our lives. And when you spend time in the Bible, you may be surprised at how amazing he truly is.

Chapter 12

On Sunday, January 12, 2014, I was fewer than twenty-four hours away from my release after serving 740 days in prison. From there, I would return home to Wisconsin and begin my one year of probation.

Three of us who were involved in ministry at Coleman were scheduled to leave that week, and we were each asked to speak to the congregation at our last church service. I prepared a prayer of thanksgiving for everything God had done during my time. I thanked him for teaching me so many things: how to forgive, how suffering is an opportunity for joy, and how love keeps no record of wrongs. I thanked him for giving me the power and desire to serve him well, for never failing or abandoning me, and for working all things for good every step of the way.

Several of my closest friends had already left by the time of my release, and saying goodbye to them had been tough. I never really got close to anyone after that. Many of the new inmates didn't get along, so the atmosphere of the prison became more hostile. It made the last six months go slower than I would have liked.

The night before an inmate leaves, they give away everything they purchased through the commissary—clothing, food, toiletries, shoes, etc. I let the Lord lead me in who he wanted me to bless. I gave my lightly worn sweatshirt and sweatpants to a new inmate who walked through the doors empty-handed. I gave my remaining food to inmates I knew had little support from home. I gave my shoes to a woman, and even though they didn't fit her, she promised to find an inmate with size six feet. I said goodbye to the women in my unit, as most of them had to be at their jobs by eight in the morning. We exchanged contact information and promised to stay in touch.

I lay awake most of the night, my mind reeling. I was curious if my friends had experienced the same mixed emotions that I was feeling. I wondered how my first day of freedom would feel, how long it would take to settle into a normal routine again, how my family and friends would receive me, and what might have changed over the last two years since I'd been gone. Prison had to have impacted my loved ones as much as it impacted me, and I felt terrible for what I had put everyone through. More questions than answers dashed through my mind, which was probably why I struggled to fall asleep that night.

Receiving and discharge told me to be ready as early as eight in the morning, so when I woke up, I stripped my bed, put my uniform in a mesh bag, and returned everything to the laundry room per protocol. When people are released, a big crowd of ladies often gather for their send-offs. The longer the sentence, the bigger the crowd. In my case, the opposite was true.

The only person sitting outside of receiving and discharge with me that morning was Shermeeka, or Big Meeka as she was called. Meeka and I had been next-door neighbors at one time, and we valued each other's friendship. She hung out with me while I waited on the cement bench outside the on-duty officer's door.

Normally, the office opened at 8:00 a.m., but it was dark inside, so we knew no one had arrived yet. Each passing minute felt like an eternity, and a twinge of anxiety set in. When the office lights finally turned on at eight fifteen, I took a deep breath. I turned to Meeka and gave her a simple hug goodbye, even though inmates were not supposed to touch, and tears welled in both of our eyes.

Then I knocked on the on-duty officer's door—only to have him tell me no releases were scheduled that day.

"Is this some sort of cruel joke?" I asked, quickly pulling out the documentation that stated the Bureau of Prisons was to release me that day. He asked me to sit in the waiting room outside of his office while he processed the paperwork. I paced back and forth, nervous that something had gone wrong and I'd be stuck at Coleman indefinitely. I had no idea when my ride would show up either. My phone and email access were removed the night before for security reasons, so I had no way of contacting them if there was a delay. I had no control over the situation, yet I was a mere twenty-five yards away from freedom.

When I stepped back into the room about thirty minutes later, my counselor and another guard were inside. It turned out that the first officer had yet to settle in and look at the day's schedule, which is why he was clueless about my release.

From the office, I could see out the front door of the prison, and their heads turned to see what I was staring at in the parking lot.

"They didn't," I said in awe. But oh yes, they did. A white stretch limousine, the same vehicle in which Edward Lewis rescued Vivian in the movie *Pretty Woman*, awaited me. A rear window rolled down, and I saw my daughter Jenny's face for the first time in more than two years.

"That's what I'm talking about!" my counselor said excitedly. "My girls in F4 go out in style!"

Not only had God told me I would be released on early parole (seven months and one day early, to be exact), but the end of the chapter from Max Lucado's book had also read, "You are going home in style!" My assignment had finally come to an end.

The rules of Coleman dictated that inmates being released were not to show or express anything out of the ordinary, so I walked toward the limo as calmly as I could. Smiling ear to hear, I held my Bible in the air. Jenny hopped out and ran toward me, hugging me tighter than ever before, a daughter received into the arms of her loving mother, in the same way God welcomes us into his loving arms, encircling us with the light and love of Christ.

"It's over, Jenny," I told her as tears streamed down her face. "It's finally over." We held on to each other, not wanting to let go.

A sign hung out the window of the limo: "Welcome Home, My Faithful Loving Daughter," along with the phrase "Receive it! Speak it! Believe it!" When I crawled into the limo, I found five of my friends wearing purple T-shirts with words matching those on the sign. They also wore red, white, and blue leis and had decorated the inside of the limo with streamers.

I was so focused on my daughter, my friends, and our excitement that I forgot to take the ceremonial drive around the parking lot to wave goodbye to all the inmates. Not to mention the fact that I couldn't wait to get off prison property. We drove down I-75 toward Tampa and took one of the first exits to get breakfast, only to end up at the same McDonald's I had visited twice while chained and shackled. Without a care in the world, I stepped out of the limo to take in the sunshine and warm weather. I was free.

My friends and Jenny asked me how I wanted to spend my first day of freedom, and I knew exactly what I wanted to do. I wanted to head to St. James United Methodist Church in Tampa to thank God for what he had done in me, for me, and through me. It was also time to thank the special women who embarked on this part of my journey. Without their love and support, it would have been significantly lonelier and so much more difficult.

I felt God put Philippians 1:7–8 on my heart to share these verses with the women.

It is right that I should feel as I do about all of you, for you have a special place in my heart. You share with me the special favor of God, both in my imprisonment and in defending and confirming the truth of the Good News. God knows how much I love you and long for you with the tender compassion of Christ Jesus.

After sharing some additional testimony with the women, we jumped back into the limo and headed to St. Petersburg for lunch.

We had a wonderful time, and trust me when I say I will never take anything for granted ever again.

A party in my honor was planned for later that evening, so we returned to Tampa mid-afternoon to relax and unwind. I found myself in one of my favorite places: a bathtub of hot, steaming water. Words cannot describe how good it felt after all that time having to take rushed showers, many of which often had human excrement on the floor. Then I visited with the other women who supported me. When these ladies told me three years ago, "We do life together," they meant it. This group of willing disciples, along with my family and friends, lived out the words found in Hebrews 13:3: "Remember those in prison, as if you were there yourself."

During my 740 days in prison, I received regular visits from my spiritual support team. Nearly every day I heard my name at mail call. Some friends sent money for my commissary account; others picked up the phone when I desperately needed to hear a familiar voice. Many stayed connected via email. When I needed a word of encouragement, a hug, a shoulder to cry on, or an intercessory prayer, they were there for me, putting my needs above their own. And what does the King say in Matthew 25:40? "I tell you the truth, when you did it to one of the least of these my brothers and sisters, you were doing it to me!" These women were extensions of God's love.

The fifteen ladies who supported me did not yet know the totality of their efforts. With their help, we distributed nearly three hundred Bibles in English and Spanish and thousands of "Just One Word" Bible calendars. Hundreds more calendars reached the homes of children with incarcerated parents, and some families received Bibles too. Over two hundred copies of Ruth Ann's *Radical Power of God* books and study guides made it into the hands of inmates, teaching them how to align themselves with God's will. More than seven hundred fifty greeting cards containing Scripture and words of encouragement lifted the spirits of the women at Coleman, and over thirty-five Christian books were donated to the camp library.

Step Into Prison, Step Out in Faith

I had shared with my friends the names and numbers of inmates who never received mail, and my friends came through. Their letters not only touched hundreds of lives but, more importantly, also changed hearts. The simple gesture of sending them mail moved many inmates to tears, and they waited expectantly for the next letter from their new friend. So many inmates feel lost and forgotten or lack family support altogether. As Galatians 6:2 reads, "Share each other's burdens, and in this way obey the law of Christ." None of this would have happened had I not been in prison, and none of this would have happened without my friends' willingness to be the hands and feet of Jesus. When we calculated our collective impact during my time at Coleman, we were blown away.

We called it an evening a little after ten o'clock, and Jenny and I headed to another friend's home, where we were spending the night. Julia and her husband, Joe, greeted us warmly. Then I walked into their guest room to find that Julia had set up the room like a luxury hotel: soft, warm lighting; bath products fragranced with jasmine, blue violet, lavender, and lily of the valley; and a Godiva chocolate delicately placed on the pillow. Even better was the queen-sized, pillow-top mattress covered in Egyptian cotton sheets and a fluffy down comforter. I fell into bed feeling special and lay there for an extended time, wondering if I was dreaming. Was I truly out of prison? Eventually I fell asleep, although it was going to take some time before I got used to sleeping somewhere other than a jail cell.

When I finally crawled out of bed and made my way downstairs the next day, long after Jenny, Julia, and Joe, a newspaper and a hot, fresh cup of coffee awaited me. We visited for a while and grabbed a sandwich, and then Jenny and I made our way to Tampa International Airport to return to Milwaukee. In fewer than four hours, we would touch down in the frozen tundra of Wisconsin and travel to my parents' house for a family pizza party. We made our final descent over an icy Lake Michigan, and the snowy shoreline reminded me how blessed I was to have served my time in warm, sunny Florida.

It was close to six o'clock in the evening when we pulled up to my parents' home. The porch light was on and the front door open, as if the house itself anticipated my arrival. Our celebration began with hugs and smiles, and my family commented on my suntan and how relaxed I looked. After the initial shock wore off that I didn't look or appear to act any differently, we all picked up right where we left off. "It doesn't even feel like you were gone!" my sister marveled.

Whether or not I wanted to admit it, though, I was physically and emotionally exhausted. And the week ahead of me would be busy, to say the least. I had only one day to relax before having to return to the federal courthouse in Milwaukee to meet with my probation officer, and I had to meet with my attorneys that week too. It quickly became apparent that I had been running on adrenaline for the last two years because, within ten days of my release, my body completely broke down out of sheer exhaustion. I was sleeping eighteen hours a day and had terrible flu-like symptoms for more than ten days. Even though I successfully managed the emotional and psychological stress of my imprisonment, my body still needed to recover.

Despite my lack of energy to write about my experience, I nevertheless pushed myself to invest in a new computer and a printer. Then I was ready to begin what I was called to do in October 2011: write the book. I sat at my desk, wondering where to start. This was God's book, not mine, so I turned the job over to the Holy Spirit, letting him guide each keystroke. I often looked back on what I had written days before and wondered, *Where did that come from?* It was remarkable how God was so specific about what he wanted me to write. At times, he would take me back to a single sentence to make a seemingly minor change, but it was always a change for the better. Speaking of changes, on February 28, I must have heard God say at least a dozen times *Call Me Vivian*, which became the title of my first book.

Step Into Prison, Step Out in Faith

In March 2014, I saw my three grandsons, Nicholas, Benjamin, and Colin, for the first time since 2011. (They helped me design the logo for The Vivian Foundation.) At the time, they were twelve, eleven, and nine years old, respectively, and staying with me during their spring break.

One of the boys' favorite activities was visiting a local candy factory. After the tour, we got into the car, and I decided to record a short video of us. I said, "Okay, Romans 4:17 says to speak things that are not as if they were, so speak it over me, baby." With child-like faith, the boys called out to God on my behalf.

Confidently, Nicholas began: "One of these days something crazy will happen. You'll win a bunch of money, or you'll get a bunch of time, and there won't be any problems with your foundation, and you'll be able to set it up really easily!"

The camera panned to Colin, who said, "I think your book will turn into a hit movie, and the book will be a bestseller. It will be a good success!"

Then it was Ben's turn: "I think you will get lots of donations from other companies for your foundation cause they like the idea."

I finished the impromptu interview with this: "I receive it! I speak it! And I believe it!" Jesus reminds us in Matthew 19:26, "Humanly speaking, it is impossible. But with God everything is possible."

On Easter Sunday, God revealed himself in a mighty way. The previous night, I decided to watch *The Ten Commandments*. Near the end of the movie, I kept dozing off because it was well past my bedtime. As a result, I did not turn off my cell phone, which I routinely do each night. Bright and early on Easter Sunday morning, I woke up to a text message alert. I got out of bed and grabbed my phone to find a picture from a friend who was attending the early morning sunrise service at St. James United Methodist Church in Tampa. I quickly replied, "Beautiful, thank you!" and crawled back into bed.

Within a minute I heard another text alert. I assumed God didn't want me to go back to sleep. This text was from another girlfriend, and she sent me a nearly identical picture from the same service. I crawled back into bed again, and when text alert number three came in, I figured I might as well get up.

When I looked at the text, I realized my first friend had inadvertently sent the photo to my old phone number too. The latest text was from my previous number, and whoever had my old phone number asked, "Who is this causing me to smile early on Easter Sunday?" I sensed in my spirit this was a God thing, that he wanted me to reply because whoever was on the other end of that phone needed encouragement.

What is it that you want me to say? I silently prayed. The only thing that rose in my spirit was a verse I was quite familiar with, so I sent: "Just God! Given he never makes a mistake, this message was also intended for the person who has my old number. I love how he works! And remember God works everything for good. Keep smiling because he loves you and has a great plan for your life. Happy Easter!"

I received another response, and as only God can do, he gave me an Easter surprise I would never forget. I received a picture of an African American man waving at me and dressed in clothes that looked familiar. His response: "In prison there is not very much that makes me smile. Then u remind me that 'all things work together for good to them that love God.' Also 'For as many r led by the Spirit of God, these r sons of God and daughters. Thank you very much & u now in my prayer today. Please say a prayer for me. Clarence G. That I be one of those blessed to be released from prison this July 1."

I just stood there looking at my phone and shaking my head in disbelief. *Are you kidding me, Lord?* Having been in prison, I know an inmate should not have a cell phone. I had recently read an article on cell phone usage in prisons, and the statistics were staggering. Although a part of me wanted to respond to Clarence's text message, I had no choice but to block my old number from my phone. I was prohibited from having contact with all inmates, or else I would violate my probation. Depending on the severity of the violation (or the mood of the probation officer), I risked being sent back to Coleman for the remainder of my sentence. I met plenty of inmates who suffered this very fate, and I was not going to take any chances.

I decided to take a walk and talk to God. Over the following two hours, I could only think about what had just happened. God had just given me a photo he did not want me to forget, and I could not get this man's face out of my head. My text message obviously gave him hope. I could see it in his eyes. I looked up Clarence's case online and learned he was facing forty-eight years in jail. I prayed for Clarence and asked God what this encounter was about, and he revealed a couple of things to me.

First, he revealed that my prison ministry would go beyond children. The Vivian Foundation would provide faith-based resources for children of incarcerated parents, and there would also be an outreach program for inmates.

For quite some time, I had been praying and believing my book would open doors for speaking engagements. And I wouldn't be a bit surprised if I found myself going back to prisons to encourage others with a message of hope: "The needy will not be ignored forever; the hopes of the poor will not always be crushed" (Psalm 9:18). The world may ignore the plight of the needy, crushing any earthly hope they have. But God, the champion of the weak, promises that this will not be the case forever. Hope requires waiting for the Lord's rescue or justice. God knows our needs. He knows our tendency for despair, and he promises to never leave us. Even when others forget us, he remembers.

Think of everything that had to happen for this inmate, Clarence, to receive his Easter miracle. From a sunrise service in Tampa, Florida, a picture from Easter Sunday was inadvertently sent to the wrong number—my old phone number, which had a Wisconsin area code. Somehow this number found its way into a county jail in Mississippi. My phone had to have been turned on that morning, or I would have slept through the message. Clarence had to ask who was making him smile, and God had to tell me what to say, and, as a result, a prisoner no longer had to wonder if God was real.

In late May, God was speaking, and I was listening. These three words were repeated four times: *patience, prudence, providence.* The repetition of these words made it clear to me that this message was important.

Patience is the ability to endure difficult circumstances without giving in to negativity. It's extremely important when you embark on a spiritual journey because mending a broken heart takes time. The secrets to maintaining a good attitude while God conforms you to his image are to trust and obey. I am living proof that God works on behalf of those who wait for him. And I was beginning to believe that I really did have the "patience of a saint" as I approached year number ten of my saga.

Prudence is having good sense in dealing with practical matters. It means thinking carefully about the consequences of your decisions. Being prudent is much like being wise, careful, and cautious. I had been giving a lot of thought to what would be expected of me moving forward. God specifically told me three things: *just be yourself, always be humble, and have a gentle, quiet spirit.* That's great advice for all of us.

As I researched the definition of *providence*, I smiled. *Providence* means that God is in control. We must remember that our life's events have been arranged in such a way to bring about God's perfect plan. "'I know the plans I have for you,' says the LORD. 'They are plans for good and not for disaster, to give you a future and a hope'" (Jeremiah 29:11).

Life is all about trusting our heavenly Father. As Proverbs 3:5–6 reads, "Trust in the LORD with all your heart; do not depend on your own understanding. Seek his will in all you do, and he will show you which path to take." Why is it important to trust him?

The book of Esther has a great answer: "Who knows if perhaps you were made queen for just such a time as this?" (Esther 4:14). One thing was certain: this book and The Vivian Foundation are kingdom projects, and I trust that God will provide everything I need on his timetable, not mine.

In early June, I wrote my final restitution payment and decided to take a walk before heading to the post office. While walking, I felt God lay Matthew 5:25–26 on my heart:

> When you are on the way to court with your adversary, settle your differences quickly. Otherwise, your accuser may hand you over to the judge, who will hand you over to an officer, and you will be thrown into prison. And if that happens, you surely won't be free again until you have paid the last penny.

I looked down at the sidewalk, and what did I find but a shiny new penny. God would not allow me to move forward until I met my financial obligation.

Back in May 2012, when God told me to pray for my release, I found confidence in the verse through which he revealed that July 11 was the day I would be set free. "Ask the LORD your God for a sign of confirmation…Make it as difficult as you want—as high as heaven or as deep as the place of the dead" (Isaiah 7:11). Another appearance of the number eleven read, "Has my arm lost its power? Now you will see whether or not my word comes true!" (Numbers 11:23).

Then, when I was not physically released from prison on July 11, 2012, my son Mike simply stated, "Mom, maybe you just got the wrong year."

For years I had been praying that my former employer would forgive me and settle this case. And on Friday, July 11, 2014, less than a month after I'd mailed my final restitution payment, my attorney called me. He forwarded me an email he'd received that was timestamped that very same day, which read, "The victim, S.C.

Johnson, considers itself paid in full." I had finally been released on July 11 of all days, 3,554 days after my journey began.

However, my probation officer told me I could not set up The Vivian Foundation until my supervisory period ended on January 12, 2015. And I knew in my heart that my first day of complete freedom, January 13, 2015, would coincide with God's perfect timing. I thought back to what my grandson Nicholas had called out on my behalf—that something crazy would happen and I'd win a bunch of money or get a bunch of time, or there would be no problems with setting up the foundation. Well, he was right.

In November 2014, I received a letter in the mail from the United States District Court for the Eastern District of Wisconsin. Without my knowledge, I had become a plaintiff in a class action lawsuit against my former employer's retirement plan, and I would receive monetary compensation. I looked at the amount and could not believe my eyes. When I had no idea where the money would come from to establish The Vivian Foundation, God opened the windows of heaven and poured out a financial blessing so great it could only be described as a miracle. The hearing for the approval of this settlement had been set: January 13, 2015, my first true day of freedom.

Little did I know that God would provide me with even more because of this blessing. I chose to take the settlement as a lifetime annuity, meaning I would receive a monthly check for the rest of my life. Not knowing exactly when I would receive the first payment or how much it would be after deductions, I was thrilled when I went to the bank at the end of July to learn a deposit had been made. After taxes, the monthly annuity amount is $816.18.

That same day, I drove back to my friend Linda's home, where I was staying, to prepare for the first Vivian Foundation board meeting. I sensed in my spirit that God had something special for me.

What are you trying to tell me, Lord?

Go to the book of Deuteronomy, he answered.

Deuteronomy 8:16–18 captures the moral of my story and will serve as my heavenly reminder every month for the rest of my life that God gives us the power to succeed.

"He fed you with manna in the wilderness, a food unknown to your ancestors. He did this to humble you and test you for your own good. He did all this so you would never say to yourself, 'I have achieved this wealth with my own strength and energy.' Remember the LORD your God. He is the one who gives you power to be successful, in order to fulfill the covenant he confirmed to your ancestors with an oath."

I wept in his presence and thanked him for everything he had done for me. Then God reminded me of those three little words he spoke to me in May 2014: *patience, prudence, providence*.

In this life, we cannot be flawless, but we can strive to be as much like Christ as possible. We must separate ourselves from the world's sinful values. We must be devoted to God's wishes rather than our own and carry his love, mercy, grace, and forgiveness into the world. We must grow toward maturity that will manifest itself in words and deeds throughout our life. Just as we expect different behaviors from a baby, a child, a teenager, and an adult, God expects different behavior from us, depending on our stage of spiritual development. Consider the rich wisdom found in Romans 12.

Don't copy the behavior and customs of this world, but let God transform you into a new person by changing the way you think. Then you will learn to know God's will for you, which is good and pleasing and perfect…

God has given us different gifts for doing certain things well. So if God has given you the ability to prophesy, speak out with as much faith as God has given you. If your gift is serving others, serve them well. If you are a teacher, teach well. If your gift is to encourage others, be encouraging. If it is giving, give generously. If God has given you leadership ability, take the responsibility seriously. And if you have a gift for showing kindness to others, do it gladly.

Don't just pretend to love others. Really love them. Hate what is wrong. Hold tightly to what is good. Love each other with genuine affection, and take delight in honoring each other...

Never pay back evil with more evil. Do things in such a way that everyone can see you are honorable. Do all that you can to live in peace with everyone.

Dear friends, never take revenge. Leave that to the righteous anger of God. For the Scriptures say, "I will take revenge; I will pay them back," says the LORD...

Don't let evil conquer you, but conquer evil by doing good. (vv. 2, 6–10, 17–19, 21)

It all came together exactly how God said it would. All the way back in February 2009, God made me a promise—a promise he would keep: "I will never fail you. I will never abandon you" (Hebrews 13:5). Like Abraham, when there was no reason to hope, I believed this journey was part of my divine destiny. I never wavered in believing God's promises and completed each assignment regardless of its difficulty. I have been strengthened in faith, which "shows the reality of what we hope for; it is the evidence of things we cannot see" (Hebrews 11:1). And because of my faith and God's unfailing love, my heart was transformed.

First Corinthians 13:13 tells us that "three things will last forever—faith, hope, and love—and the greatest of these is love." All things are possible with God if you simply have the faith to believe. Are you ready to run into the loving arms of your Savior? It's the only way to live happily ever after.

Chapter 13

During the third week of May of 2016, I traveled to Atlanta for The Vivian Foundation's first event: a three-day conference hosted by the Correctional Ministries and Chaplains Association (CMCA). The mission of the CMCA is to connect, encourage, equip, and strengthen Christians as they fulfill the Great Commission in corrections. CMCA's belief is that the power of Christ can transform the lives of the incarcerated, formerly incarcerated, and their families to strengthen communities. Their goal is to support correctional ministry professionals, volunteers, and organizations serving those affected by crime and incarceration.

Bound for Atlanta with my car packed full of ministry resources, I budgeted two days of travel time, which left me with several hours to reflect on everything that had taken place since my release from prison. If it all hadn't happened to me personally, I'm not sure that I would believe it.

Two friends of mine from Tampa, Paula and Patrice, agreed to help me with the conference. We had talked about this event for months, and none of us knew what to expect. Once all three of us had arrived, we enjoyed a nice dinner before returning to the hotel early. I felt exhausted from the drive and determined to get a good night's sleep. Tossing and turning in anticipation, I might have slept three hours at most. In the morning, we set up our table and hung our banners, and our display looked great. Spread across the table were marketing materials and books, ready and waiting to reach the hands of hundreds of attendees.

God's presence was powerful at the conference those next three days. The testimonies, tears, and personal stories of so many people touched our hearts and were evidence of God's infinite grace. I met former inmates, some of whom only recently obtained their release. One man, whom the court had wrongly convicted, spent more than half of his adult life behind bars before the declaration of his innocence.

There was Latoya, who approached our table and asked us for a big hug. I held her as she broke down in tears. She thanked me for starting The Vivian Foundation because she was one of "those kids" left homeless as a result of her mother's criminal past and incarceration. She was the only family member around to raise her younger brother, and she was still grieving and processing everything she had endured.

Then there was Miko, who was involved in re-entry programs in the Atlanta area. He poured out his heart in a way that I had never experienced. His vulnerability while sharing his pain and heartache was powerful. We could not help but feel touched by the love he received from his family and friends despite the struggles and challenges that life had thrown his way.

God opened another door for me that weekend. Best-selling author Carol Kent attended the conference as the keynote speaker. I'd read all her books and always hoped to meet her, and not only did I meet her, but I also enjoyed breakfast with her and her husband, Gene. Their life was turned upside down when their only child, Jason, committed murder and was issued a life sentence in the state of Florida.

Carol and Gene are passionate about helping inmates and their families adjust to their new normal. Together, they founded the nonprofit organization Speak Up for Hope, which benefits prisoners and their families. Carol, Gene, and I discussed many aspects of their ministry work, notably how to embrace hidden gifts that can be found amid undesirable circumstances. I listened intently to Carol's words of wisdom and knew in my heart that only God could have arranged that breakfast meeting. He was teaching me through the experiences of others, and a vast amount of knowledge was transferred to me during our brief meal together. His perfect plan was unfolding right before my eyes in a way that I had only dreamed possible.

Another highlight for me was watching Voices of Hope, a choir from the Lee Arrendale Prison. Their performance touched me to the core, and they received multiple standing ovations throughout their set. I wondered about each of their stories. I wondered about their individual crimes and sentences. I wondered what thoughts crossed their minds after enjoying a glimpse of freedom and normalcy for a few hours in the outside world. My heart broke when they left the auditorium, knowing that boarding the bus to return to prison was the last thing they wanted to do.

As the weekend progressed, I met countless other men and women committed to helping inmates, former inmates, and their families. One woman's story stands out in my memory. She introduced herself as Scottie Barnes, a woman who was in her seventies and a child of an incarcerated parent. That weekend, CMCA was formally recognizing Scottie and her husband, Jack, for their tireless years of service in corrections ministry. Their personal ministry, Forgiven Ministry, was based out of Taylorsville, North Carolina. It was established as a 501c3 nonprofit organization in October of 2000, but its story began in 1995, when Scottie and Jack were running a thriving business in Taylorsville. Busy following their own plans and pursuits in life, Scottie admitted that she and Jack had never asked God about his plan for them.

Then one day, the chaplain of the local prison in their small town walked into their boutique and asked Scottie if she would speak at the prison's Sunday night worship service. *I never intended to go back to prison*, Scottie thought. *I visited my father behind bars since the age of four, virtually all my life.*

Scottie looked at the chaplain and said, "I really don't have anything to say."

With a look of sincerity, the chaplain asked, "Wasn't your daddy saved before he served his last prison term as a drug kingpin?"

Scottie remembered Matthew 25:36: "I was in prison, and you visited me." Scottie agreed to visit the local prison, and when she spoke, her testimony unfolded with such an anointing that she knew she was in the presence of God at work and doing his perfect will. She felt God calling her and Jack into ministry to help children who experienced the same type of loneliness and separation that she had.

Given the hundreds of thousands of lives that Forgiven Ministry has since touched, we are all grateful that Scottie and Jack answered God's call. Forgiven Ministry also participates in "One Day with God," a program that reunites children with their incarcerated parents and guides them through a series of fun, spiritual-based activities.

God was beginning to open the doors he wanted me to walk through, one with the help of an Oklahoma senator. It was becoming increasingly apparent that God was serious about the things he called me to do. All these ministries were well established and successful inside of prisons throughout the United States and beyond.

After the conference, I drove to Titusville to visit the Prison Book Project. Ray Hall started the Prison Book Project more than twenty-five years ago, and he and his wife, Joyce, have been instrumental in touching the lives of the incarcerated by shipping millions of Christian books into nearly three thousand jails and prisons throughout the country. Joining me on my visit was my friend Ruth Ann Nylen. We loaded her vehicle with thousands of her books to donate to the Prison Book Project.

Upon our arrival, I opened the glass door that bore the Prison Book Project's logo and could not stop smiling. I was finally going to meet Ray and Joyce and thank the people who sent me the NLT red-letter Bible while I was incarcerated. I had talked to them on numerous occasions after my release, as The Vivian Foundation supports their ministry. I also forwarded additional copies of my book to their warehouse.

What Ray and Joyce did not know was that we also had business to discuss. The red-letter Bible that was sent to me on behalf of the Prison Book Project was used to develop our "Just One Word Bible Reading Plan." After sharing this news with them, I asked Ray how many Bible reading plans he thought their ministry could help us distribute. Confidently, he replied, "Ten thousand." Our hearts could not help but be touched by the impact that one red-letter Bible had on all of us.

Ray broke down in tears as he realized the ripple effect of his ministry's hard work, which began in 1994. After touring a corrections facility, he saw the need to provide higher quality resources than what was available in the jail library. Ray visited a number of churches that responded to his plea for help, and the Prison Book Project was born. Today, with the help of Christian publishers, authors, volunteers, and generous donors, the Prison Book Project has become one of the most successful prison book ministries in the country.

In June of 2016, just months after *Call Me Vivian* launched, the time came for me to walk back through the doors of Coleman. But this time I was returning as a guest speaker for their annual Woman 2 Woman conference, not as an inmate. Two and a half years had passed since my release, and in that time, I had become an author, the president of a nonprofit organization, and a motivational speaker. I was one of two former inmates invited to speak at Coleman's annual Woman 2 Woman conference and share my testimony. The themes of the conference were embracing all that God has for us, standing on his promises, and demonstrating how our faith in God can truly move mountains.

How would I feel when I drove onto the compound? I wasn't sure. The landscape of Coleman was familiar, but the emotions could not have been more different. One thing I was all too aware of was that I was returning to the largest federal prison in the country to do exactly what God called me to do: inspire inmates with a message of hope.

I parked my car, and the first building to catch my attention was F4, my old unit. The inmates were expecting me, so it was not a surprise when I saw a few of them standing on the porch and waving. I unloaded the car and approached the front entrance, peering through the double doors. One of my friends stood on the grounds, and I spotted the chaplain in the visiting room. I opened the door, wheeled in a cart full of books, and much to my surprise, my arms went into the air, and I began praying in my prayer language. As strange as this sounds, the pure joy I felt in that moment was unlike anything I had ever experienced. The only feeling I can liken it to is making a game-winning shot at the sound of the buzzer.

I walked the entire length of the visiting room with my arms in the air and greeted Chaplain Garcia with a big hug. The doors opened forty-five minutes ahead of the conference, and many of the inmates who knew me dropped by beforehand to say hello. I spent quality time with each of them, sharing words of wisdom and encouragement. Given I had attended events like this before, I knew what to expect, and I knew it was going to be a fun afternoon.

The women filed into the visiting room, and I recognized another familiar face: Miss Elaine. Elaine lived in F4 with me and had been incarcerated for over twenty years. The moment our eyes met, our tears began to flow. During my two years at Coleman, I shared many books with Elaine. She was always happy to receive something new to read. She and I had a little tradition too. Elaine would not accept a book from me without first encouraging me to sign it. "You have to practice," she'd say. For her, I ended up autographing dozens of books that I had no hand in writing! Elaine closely examined *Call Me Vivian* and The Vivian Foundation banners flanking the podium. She kept shaking her head and smiling, remembering all the times we spoke about the book and the work God would do.

The conference lasted about two hours in length and included praise and worship by the Coleman Choir, corporate prayer, a performance by the Coleman Dance Team, and presentations by two other guest speakers. Both ladies spoke of their respective challenges in life and how you can overcome anything with the power and love of God.

When the time came for me to speak, I was in my element. I had stepped up to that microphone on three other occasions during my incarceration. Toastmasters was one of many programs offered to inmates, and I took advantage of it. Our meetings were held on Thursday evenings, and these gatherings were always well attended. Many women wanted to develop their learning, speaking, and leadership skills, and the program allowed many of us an opportunity to speak in front of a group and talk about our personal lives without feeling judged.

I spoke during these meetings on numerous occasions. My first speech was about what I wanted to be when I grew up. My second speech was titled "Service with a Smile," and my last message was "Get out of Jail Free!" I enjoyed researching the respective subject matter, incorporating Scripture into my speeches, and creatively delivering my messages, although I always lost points for exceeding the allotted time limit. Do you think God set a time limit on Jesus' sermons? Giving God all the glory takes more than five to seven minutes! Still, I knowingly took the hit every time because I knew what I had to say was important.

My time to become a real motivational speaker arrived, so I turned myself over to the Holy Spirit. Many of the women I had befriended were still serving their time, so I was able to share the lessons I had learned at Coleman while the Lord prepared my heart for my call to ministry. I shared the lesson found in Romans 4:17 to speak things that are not as if they were. Then I connected that lesson to all the things that many of us had spoken into existence with *Call Me Vivian* and The Vivian Foundation. I reminded each of them that God has a great plan for their life, and while they are at Coleman, God's purpose for them is to mend their broken hearts and prepare them for whatever comes next.

"Don't ever give up hope," I stressed. "God is a God of the impossible. If he can do this for me, he can do it for you!"

The conference came to a close, and I gifted a book to each attendee. Then I signed autographs for close to thirty minutes, including one for Miss Elaine. All that practice finally paid off!

Returning to the compound was indeed special. I never realized how much the spiritual training ground of Coleman meant to me. It was my home for 740 days after all. For two years, it was where I received guidance from the Holy Spirit, which prepared me for my ministry calling. It may have been prison for the other 500 inmates who were incarcerated with me, but for me it was the place where God did his best work. It's where he transformed my heart and taught me about true love. As I exited the building and returned to my car for the drive back to Wisconsin, I knew with certainty that, like Queen Esther, I had been made precisely for a time such as this.

The Lord's purpose for us on this journey is simple: God wants us to have an intimate relationship with his Son, Jesus Christ, and to serve others in love. To believe in God means to put our trust, confidence, and faith in Jesus because he is the only One who can save us. We must surrender our will and put Jesus Christ in charge of our earthly life and eternal destiny. We must also believe that God's Word is true and reliable. And when you ask Jesus into your heart, you gain a comforting friend known as the Holy Spirit, who leads you in all truth.

God is always at work, readying our circumstances, because he wants to bless us. But we must be willing to wait for his perfect plan to unfold. He will often first purify our motives and prepare our hearts. Other times, he protects us before blessing us. God never makes a mistake; waiting on him will always provide awesome testimony relative to his love, goodness, faithfulness, and provision.

Step Into Prison, Step Out in Faith

I could relate to so many Bible characters. Like the apostle Paul, I have moved around a lot, and I guess I really did do some of my best work in prison. However, the character I admired most was Joseph, and his story in the Bible is one of my favorites. Joseph was the favored son of his father and betrayed by his brothers, which led to his unjust incarceration of thirteen years. His journey included hardship, humility, and pain, yet God used Joseph's adversities to prepare him and to fulfill a greater story.

As wonderful as God's preparation of us can be, it can also be equally painful and difficult. That's because God brings our sore spots to our attention not only to make us aware of the changes that we need to make but also to teach us to rely on him for strength. That's why things sometimes get worse before they get better. When you hit rock bottom, God is truly the only person who can help.

We are all Joseph. It doesn't matter if you are a man or a woman, young or old, behind bars or roaming free; we are all set apart for God's divine purposes. God wants you to know his assignment so that you can live an intentional, meaningful, purposeful life. You might not see or understand what he is up to, but just like he prepared Joseph, he is preparing you for work in his kingdom too.

Chapter 14

Scottie Barnes of Forgiven Ministry was in Raleigh when she called me, overcome with emotion after she left the North Carolina Correctional Institution for Women (NCCIW). I was scheduled to speak at this same facility the following week for Forgiven Ministry's "One Day with God" event, a two-day camp reuniting incarcerated parents with their children.

"I have never seen a book like *Call Me Vivian* so highly requested by inmates and staff, Katie," Scottie said. "I can't wait for you to meet all these ladies. God is doing amazing things with your testimony. We're so excited for your visit."

Forgiven Ministry's mission is to meet the spiritual, physical, and emotional needs of current and former inmates, their children, and their families by tangibly showing the love of Christ. One of those ways is through their "One Day with God" camps, and forty women at NCCIW had earned the privilege to attend camp that year because of their good behavior.

As I waited inside the Milwaukee airport to board my flight to Raleigh, God clearly told me, *It is time to be bold!* His command prompted me to open my Bible and turn to Joshua 1:9, which happened to be the same verse God had given me when I was flown to the county jail in Chickasaw, Oklahoma. Joshua 1:9 reads, "This is my command—be strong and courageous! Do not be afraid or discouraged. For the LORD your God is with you wherever you go." But nothing could have prepared me for what I would experience at "One Day with God."

Step Into Prison, Step Out in Faith

It was my first visit to Raleigh, and I secretly hoped I would have enough time to visit Durham and Chapel Hill, mere miles away, to soak in the Duke–North Carolina basketball rivalry I'd come to love. Scottie and her husband, Jack, picked me up at the airport, and to my delight and surprise, the chaplain of NCCIW stepped out of the vehicle to greet me too. I felt like a celebrity! We all exchanged hugs before driving to West South Street, where we approached the home belonging to Robert and Deborah Nash, our host family for the weekend. Those of us who were staying with the Nash family included Scottie, Jack, a volunteer, and myself.

The Nash's frame home, built in 1935, featured an inviting front porch, stunning interior design, and a white picket fence. The couple had lived there for years and welcomed us with remarkable warmth. They woke up early to prepare coffee and breakfast for us, generously meeting every one of our needs. They even introduced me to toasted Asiago cheese bread with butter and homemade jam (I still think of them whenever I enjoy Asiago bread!). God had clearly blessed the Nash family with the spiritual gift of serving because I immediately felt at home.

With a full schedule ahead of us on Friday and Saturday, I turned in early that Thursday evening, hoping for a restful night of sleep. I ended up tossing and turning all night though—too excited from anticipating what God had planned.

The number of volunteers needed to host an event like this required assistance from a local church. Christ Our King Community Church, located near the prison, would help transport volunteers and children to the facility while caregivers remained at the church. But since the children would not arrive until Saturday morning, the mothers would be the focus on Friday.

We pulled into the prison's parking lot on Friday morning just before seven. The early start gave us extra time to check in and set everything up prior to the mothers' arrival at nine. We passed through metal detectors, and then a guard escorted us to the gymnasium where the event would take place. I realized we'd be on a basketball court and had to smile. "One Day with God" was one of the biggest events in which I'd participated to date, and only God could have orchestrated it to unfold inside a gym, lining me up next to other speakers who shared my passion for the game.

When it comes to sports, basketball was my first love even though I was technically a better softball player. Way back in 1975, when I was a senior at Saint Catherine's High School in Racine, our team played in Wisconsin's first-ever Independent Schools Athletic Association State Basketball Championship game, which also happened to be the first state championship ever held for girls. As captain of the team and a starting guard, I had such high hopes for us. Sadly, we lost by three points and finished the season as the state's runner-up. I was the only senior on the team, which meant I was the only one who wouldn't get a second chance to win it all the next year. I took the loss hard.

Sure enough, the very next season, my former team went undefeated and won the coveted Gold Ball. I sat in the bleachers and watched them celebrate their victory. I was genuinely happy for them, but internally I struggled with it. I asked the same question over and over in my head: *Why was I the only one who didn't get a second chance?* I honestly did not come to grips with that heartbreaking loss for years, but it didn't extinguish my love for the game either. March Madness remains my favorite time of the year, and I've had the privilege to attend both the men's and women's Final Four Championship games. Nevertheless, that Friday morning, as I stood on a basketball court inside the largest state prison in North Carolina, I understood why I had to wait for my second chance; it had manifested itself in a way that I never could have imagined.

Temperatures hovered near ninety degrees, so the gymnasium's windows were open, and large fans circulated copious amounts of hot air around us. I was confident in my ability to share my testimony, but between the heat and my long pants and T-shirt, one thing was certain: I was going to have to lean on God for the strength to get through the weekend.

Step Into Prison, Step Out in Faith

Forty women entered the gym, and I felt an immediate pull toward each one of them. Common prison protocol required a head count when they arrived, and it brought back memories of my own time in prison. Since my release, I had somehow managed to suppress those memories, but I almost instinctively jumped in line with them. Some things you never forget.

The inmates and volunteers formed a big circle in the gym to open the day with prayer. The inmates formed a semicircle on one side, and the volunteers formed a complementary configuration directly across from them. A prompting in my spirit led me to jog to the inmates' side. The chaplain led the prayer, and I was so overcome with God's presence that all I could do was cry. Everything that God had promised throughout this journey was playing out right before my eyes, and quite honestly, it was overwhelming.

As the schedule and agenda dictated, I remained in the gymnasium with the women during praise and worship. While other presenters facilitated the inmates' preparation time with Scripture study, Scottie and I headed to the Robbins Unit to visit other inmates. The Robbins Unit housed two infirmaries, both of which we would visit. Many of these women had received copies of *Call Me Vivian* ahead of time and were looking forward to meeting me and having their books signed. Whenever I'm asked to sign a book, I feel overwhelmed in the best way possible. It's joyful and flattering, of course, but those moments also remind me that God is using my testimony—and me. It's a powerful reminder that I am valued in the kingdom of heaven.

The elevator door slid open, and the sight of inmates resting in hospital beds, locked inside cells, caught me off guard, and something shifted deep inside my soul. I felt as though I were seeing their circumstances through the eyes of Jesus. I no longer saw inmates; I saw women of all races, ethnicities, sizes, and shapes as one. God was showing me that these were his sick and wounded lambs in desperate need of love. His presence reminded me of 1 Samuel 16:7: "The LORD doesn't see things the way you see them. People judge by outward appearance, but the LORD looks at the heart." It also reminded me of the time during my incarceration when God told me, *This journey has never been about who was right or wrong; this journey has always been about your heart.*

I greeted each woman individually, offering a hug or handshake. I listened to their stories, however brief, and told each of them that God loves them. Some were unable to leave their rooms, so I approached their doorways to make each woman feel special and to encourage her. We also left behind small gifts from The Vivian Foundation, and for a short time, I truly believed these women forgot where they were. Two ladies from an organization called Dribble for Destiny had accompanied us to the infirmary and displayed their basketball-handling abilities. We played games with inmates who were able to participate, and their laughs and smiles were priceless. We prepared to leave, and an inmate asked if she could pray for me.

"Of course," I replied.

"God," she started, "I ask in the mighty name of Jesus that you take Katie's book to all the ends of the earth for your glory. Amen."

Not only her kindness but also the kindness of everyone else touched me. We were off to the next unit, where we repeated the same activities. God even allowed me to minister to some of the staff members who read my book and wanted to meet me. Scottie had been right; the Lord was doing amazing things with my testimony. After exiting the second infirmary, Scottie pulled me aside toward another building.

"We have one more place to visit before heading back to our event," Scottie said. "Katie, it's time to visit death row."

When I least expected it, God had opened the door for me to minister to women who, because of their crimes, were sentenced to death. Scottie had visited these ladies before, but this was my first time. According to the Death Penalty Information Center, "Around 2,500 prisoners currently face execution in the United States."[20] We don't hear much about executions, but at least one is scheduled every month. Lethal injection is most used, but other methods are authorized as well. Trust me when I tell you that nothing can prepare you for a visit like this.

I took a deep breath before walking toward the elevator and heading upstairs. Two guards sat at their command post, expecting our arrival. After completing proper security protocol, the first steel door opened and closed behind us and then a second one. Then I stepped inside a space that few people ever experience.

Dressed in maroon jumpsuits and awaiting our arrival were all three death row inmates: Blanche, Carlette, and Christina. Blanche, also known as "the Black Widow," was in her mid-eighties and the oldest among them. She had been on death row since November of 1990 and was convicted of murdering one of her husbands and a boyfriend by slipping arsenic into their food. She's suspected to have killed others in the same manner. Given her death sentence, she never faced trial for the other murders or the attempted murder of another husband.

Carlette was in her fifties and a former home health care worker. The facility had received Carlette on April 1, 1999, after she kidnapped an eighty-six-year-old woman, forced her to withdraw money from her bank account, and then murdered her. At the time of the woman's murder, Carlette was thirty-four years old. The youngest death row inmate, Christina, was in her late thirties and had been on death row since July 2000. A member of a local gang, Christina kidnapped and murdered two women at random as part of her gang initiation. A third victim had been left for dead but survived the attack.

My eyes cautiously looked beyond the spot where we stood to survey the women's living quarters: seven cells, a common area used for eating and visiting, and a small, secure concrete patio that the inmates were permitted to use for one hour each day. What I found particularly interesting was their view, which overlooked the prison's chapel. I paused. Jesus was confirming to me once again that, regardless of their crimes, I had to see these women through his eyes. As 1 John 1:8–9 reads, "If we claim we have no sin, we are only fooling ourselves and not living in the truth. But if we confess our sins to him, he is faithful and just to forgive us our sins and to cleanse us from all wickedness."

We spent a fair amount of time visiting, and each woman received a copy of *Call Me Vivian*. They showed me their handiwork, as they all learned to crochet and spent a fair amount of time crafting. It brought me back to my time at Coleman and reminded me of the artistic talent of so many inmates there too. I wondered if these women had missed their calling. It was clear that we all enjoyed our time together, and all too soon it was time to say goodbye. I enjoyed a long embrace with Blanche, then Christina, and finally Carlette, who sobbed in my arms and told me she did not think she could endure another day.

While exiting through the same set of steel doors through which we entered, I thanked God for this opportunity. Given the state of my heart at that moment, I understood that the Lord had brought me to another level of my ministry call. I let out a deep sigh while leaving that part of the facility, grateful and humbled that he had chosen me for such an assignment.

Scottie and I returned to the gymnasium and grabbed sandwiches for lunch. Meanwhile, the inmates were busy making crafts and preparing gift bags for their children. They all wore their bright green "One Day with God" shirts. Volunteers performed a ceremony called "The Crowning of the Mothers," during which each mother received a tiara and listened to volunteers reiterate how special they were. Self-esteem and confidence are often greatly lacking among inmates, so it was important to boost their morale and lift their spirits, which would hopefully carry over into the following day. A guest singer entertained the women, and Forgiven Ministry showed a powerful video captured by ABC's *Nightline* from a "One Day with God" camp that had taken place at another facility to help prepare the women for what to expect on Saturday.

Then the time came for me to speak, and I was allotted forty-five minutes to share my testimony. I made sure to share a video from Candice Glover's award-winning performance on *American Idol* in 2012, when she sang "When You Believe." I had watched that season finale while incarcerated at Coleman, and I knew that evening, as I sat in federal prison, that everything God had promised would come true. As the video started and Candice's voice rang out through the gymnasium, emotions flooded through me once again. The lyrics were so timely, and my life is proof that miracles truly can happen when you believe. I finished my afternoon speech, but I could sense that it lacked something. I asked the volunteers for candid feedback and made revisions for my evening speech, which would be in front of even more inmates.

We ate a quick dinner before the officers opened the doors to the gym, and more than one hundred fifty inmates came to hear my story. Each attendee received a Bible reading plan and a copy of *Call Me Vivian*. Although I had revised my evening speech, I closed my portfolio when I reached the podium and told God, *This is your show. You are going to have to take over because I'm running on empty.*

For the next hour, the inmates laughed and cried as the Holy Spirit spoke through me. I cannot even tell you what I said because they were not my words but truly the words of God. I handed off the microphone to the gals from Dribble for Destiny. Hugs and high fives abounded afterward, and the volunteers told me they, too, were moved by what they had witnessed. Nearly one hundred women gave their lives to Christ that night. Again, I was exactly where I was supposed to be. Exhausted, Scottie, Jack, and I headed back to the Nash's home. I had never felt so spiritually, emotionally, and physically drained in my life.

Saturday morning was another early wake-up call. It was a warm, sunny day in Raleigh, and with temperatures in the eighties and even more bodies inside the gymnasium, it was certain to be another hot one. Instead of heading directly to the prison, we first headed to the church to greet the children.

As kids arrived and settled in, I met Sandra Kearns from On Wings Like a Dove Ministry. Her ministry partners with Forgiven Ministry to distribute treasure boxes filled with coloring books, crayons, word search puzzles, and other activities to the children. Caregivers received gift bags too. Some of the kids enjoyed the snacks we had set out while others had their faces painted. A handful of the kids were outgoing and quick to share about themselves. Others were more introspective, and you could see the apprehension that lined their faces. Believe it or not, some children meet their mother or father for the first time during "One Day with God" camps. Regardless, we all made sure to be patient and supportive as they adjusted.

We needed to board the bus and leave the church at nine o'clock to allow enough time for the children to be processed at the prison. Caregivers had to remain at the church, as security concerns prohibited them from entering the prison. Once each child was successfully processed, they entered the waiting room with their designated volunteer. Unlike the other volunteers, my assignment did not involve working with a child. I would participate in the morning events, but in the afternoon, I would return to the church to speak to the caregivers and then travel back to the prison toward the end of the program to say goodbye.

After processing, volunteers escorted the children to the gymnasium, which meant they had to walk across the compound and past other inmates. The kids had full visibility of the prison surroundings, and I wondered what thoughts crossed their minds. I hoped and prayed they were focused on one thing: reuniting with their mothers.

The music began, and the mothers stood at the baseline on one side of the basketball court. One by one, their children's names were announced, and then their child would enter the gym through the double doors and run the length of the floor into their mother's arms. The clapping that ensued with the announcement of each name continued until every child and mother had their time to shine. Many mothers welcomed more than one child into her arms, leaving them tangled up in a pile on the floor together, all wrapped up in one big mama-bear hug. I ran out of tissues before all the children had reunited with their mothers. The joy inside that gym was tangible and a feeling I will never forget.

One of the most painful parts of the day, however, was having to tell one of the mothers that her child was unable to attend. We did not know why. She began to break down, and I felt a tug in my heart to go over to her, take her in my arms, and hold her tightly, comforting her as best I could. I held her face in my hands and looked at her red-rimmed eyes, telling her we needed to trust God even though it hurt. We do not know the Lord's thoughts or understand his plans, but we do know that God works all things for good (Micah 4:12; Romans 8:28).

The decibels in the gym rose with the temperature and the excitement, and it was time for the fun and games to begin. Dribble for Destiny entertained the families with basketball relay games. Everyone celebrated missed birthdays with cake and a booming rendition of "Happy Birthday." While the inmates were enjoying time with their children, Scottie introduced me to Patricia, a woman Scottie had previously told me about.

Patricia had been on death row for more than twenty-five years for murdering her husband, and through an appeal, the court commuted her sentence to life in prison. That ruling meant she could remain with the general population rather than the death row inmates, but she would never be released from prison.

What Scottie had initially told me about Patricia was that *Be Still and Know*, a coloring book from BroadStreet Publishing that The Vivian Foundation had donated to the facility, had saved Patricia's life. When I met Patricia at "One Day with God," I asked if she felt comfortable sharing her experience with me, and she was happy to oblige.

I stood at the officer's station, waiting for my signature on my work sheet. An officer had placed her mug on the counter and started yelling at me to get away from her coffee.

"I'm not touching it," I said.

She shouted back, "But you are breathing."

I told her I wish I wasn't. I returned to my laundry room job, thinking of all the reasons why I'd be better off dead. The seed of suicide had been planted.

Over the next four months, I sought counseling from a mental health professional and kept my weekly appointments, but the seed grew into an obsession. I felt useless to God, myself, and others. There was no hope and no future, and I was helpless to change it. I withdrew from all religious activities, and my eating, sleeping, and social habits changed. I just wanted to be alone. Thoughts of suicide prevailed over everything that required my attention: conversation, reading, TV. I identified with Jonah in the belly of the fish: "I went down to the bottom of the mountains" (Jonah 2:6 GNT). You can't get deeper and darker than that.

I had my plan, set a date, gave away my possessions, wrote a note, and was counting down the days of my final week when I decided to ask the chaplain about the theological consequences of suicide. She insisted on seeing me the next day and every day that week. When she gave me a coloring book and pencils, I thought, *Thanks, but I have no intention of returning to a childhood pastime.* Still, I paged through it, and Psalm 22:19 caught my attention: "LORD, do not be far from me. You are my strength; come quickly to help me" (NIV). I realized I had not called on God.

I began coloring and rereading Scripture. After a while, I realized I wasn't thinking about death but about what color I should use next. In the following days, I would color whenever suicidal thoughts invaded. And the more complicated and detailed the picture was, the more I concentrated on it. My "date" passed, and I'm still here.

Because of Patricia's story and with God's help, over seventeen hundred inmates at NCCIW were blessed with Majestic Expressions coloring books compliments of BroadStreet Publishing, The Vivian Foundation, and Forgiven Ministry, Inc. About a month after "One Day with God," Patricia sent me a letter, telling me she had started her own ministry inside the walls of the prison and had already helped four other inmates battling suicidal thoughts. Instead of waking up in tears from feelings of hopelessness, Patricia woke up in tears over the awesomeness of God.

"One Day with God" came to a close, and I stood outside the prison gate, watching the mothers and their children release balloons into the sky. It was their last activity together before saying goodbye and returning to the caregivers who waited in the prison parking lot. I watched every child, regardless of their age, fall into the arms of their trusted caregivers, sobbing over having said goodbye to their mothers. My heart swelled with compassion in a way I had never experienced before. Tears rolled down my cheeks, and I thanked God for allowing me to be a part of the event.

That weekend taught me a powerful, intense lesson in compassion and empathy. Most of us liken empathy to putting ourselves in someone else's shoes, and in my case, I had worn those women's shoes. I understood their feelings and identified with them all too well. The thing is, though, that empathy doesn't always look the same. Psychologists define three types of empathy: cognitive, emotional, and compassionate. Cognitive empathy is the ability to put yourself in someone else's shoes and see things from their perspective. It's "empathy by thought" rather than feeling. "Emotional empathy is when you literally feel the other person's emotions alongside them. It's good because it means that you "readily understand and feel other people's emotions," but it can also become overwhelming.

Compassionate empathy is when we feel someone's pain and take action to help—and that's what ministry work is all about.[21]

First Peter 3:8 says we are to all be of one mind, and that one mind Peter is referring to is the mind of Christ. According to Peter, oneness is created by treating one another with compassion, love, tenderness, and courtesy—four qualities that lie at the heart of empathy. That's why we must develop a deep understanding of who people are, how they became who they are, what they know, how they learned it, how they feel, and why they feel that way.

On April 11, 2021, the Lord told me, *The true mileage we travel is based on the strength of our resolve.* Our resolve is our determination—our relentless pursuit toward a difficult goal despite whatever obstacles may stand in our way. Tough, painful, difficult times strengthened not only my confidence but also my determination to succeed. True determination is a spiritual quality, and it's acquired by yielding to both the Holy Spirit and God's will.

By his divine power, God has given us everything we need to live a godly life. We have received all this by coming to know him, the one who called us to himself by means of his marvelous glory and excellence. And because of his glory and excellence, he has given us great promises. These promises enable us to share in his divine nature and escape the worlds' corruption caused by human desires (2 Peter 1:3–4).

In October 2022, my book *Vivian's Call*, the sequel to *Call Me Vivian*, launched, and God opened a big door for me with an opportunity of a lifetime. Janet Parshall, nationally syndicated radio talk show host of *In the Market with Janet Parshall* on Moody Radio, which has more than one million listeners on any given day, asked to interview me. I certainly didn't see that one coming.

My friends could hardly believe their ears when I shared the news with them. We have all listened to Janet's podcasts for years. I had one week to prepare for the live, hour-long interview, and I asked God to lead me in selecting portions of my books to share. I felt confident that everything would go according to his plan.

Janet's questions were tough and personal, yet the time flew by. When the familiar closing music began to play, I listened to Janet's parting words, feeling humbled by the experience: "See, friends, I told you these are my favorite conversations on radio. If God can work in and through Katie to birth a ministry that impacts the lives of people in prison and the children of incarcerated parents, imagine what he can do in, for, and through you."

If God could transform me, he can transform you too. In Romans 2:11, God tells us he has no favorites. We are all sinners who fall short of God's glorious standard, but his grace saves us.

It took me a long time to realize that the goal of our spiritual journey is not to become the perfect Christian. Our goal is to develop an intimate relationship with Christ, and that takes time. It is a slow and delicate process that requires a lot of patience. We tend to worry about how fast we grow, but God is more concerned about our strength and character *as* we grow. Consider the wisdom in James 1:2–4.

> Dear brothers and sisters, when troubles of any kind come your way, consider it an opportunity for great joy. For you know that when your faith is tested, your endurance has a chance to grow. So let it grow, for when your endurance is fully developed, you will be perfect and complete, needing nothing.

Notice that James does not say *if* trouble comes your way; he says *when* trouble comes your way. We simply cannot know the depth of our character until we face hardships, but we must remember that God uses those hardships for his glory and our good.

Our spiritual journey has always been about our heart: "The LORD doesn't see things the way you see them. People judge by outward appearance, but the LORD looks at the heart" (1 Samuel 16:7). We cannot begin to change and grow until we realize that we cannot reach the life we desire by ourselves. We need to be empowered by God's love by inviting Jesus into our hearts and letting the Holy

Spirit guide our life. Will we fail along the way? Absolutely. But God uses our failures as teaching tools.

When it comes to your unique spiritual journey, it is precisely that: *your* journey. You are not competing against anyone else; you are in a spiritual race against yourself, running toward the goal of conforming to the image of Christ. And as long as you continue to seek him along the way, he will reveal all the special talents and abilities he planted within you. And he will use those talents and abilities to call you into places you never could have imagined to accomplish things you never thought yourself capable of doing. Your job, then, is to walk in obedience. To trust God and his perfect plan with all your heart. He will lead you; he always does. And not only will he lead you in your journey, but he may also show you your true purpose in life along the way.

Acknowledgments

To my mom, dad, brothers, sisters, kids, grandkids, and their families: Thank you for your unconditional love throughout this journey. God truly works all things for good for those who love him and are called to his purpose. God's many blessings bestowed upon our family are a testament to his grace and goodness.

To my loyal friends: When others walked out, you walked in and stayed. Your love, care, and concern are examples of true friendship.

To the remarkable women at Camp Coleman: I thank each and every woman I met during my incarceration. You taught me how to give God the glory and renew my mind in Christ. Together we anointed doors, hit our knees in prayer, shook off the dust, and worshiped face down. Thank you to those who delivered prophetic words to me. Your obedience fueled my passion for writing and helped me stay the course. To my friends who kept me laughing, you are living proof that, no matter where life takes us, we can still have fun.

To the inmates who contact me: Thank you for sharing how God has used my testimony to encourage you and speak to your heart. As I carry this story to the world, please remember that each of you goes with me.

To the team at BroadStreet Publishing: Thank you for providing The Vivian Foundation with well over one hundred thousand Christian books that have been shared among prison ministries and other nonprofit organizations throughout the United States. Our partnership was part of a greater plan that only God could have orchestrated. Nina Rose, I am forever grateful for your editing expertise and God-given talent as we perfected this book. Each and every edit you made was a blessing!

To Ray and Joyce Hall and the volunteers at the Prison Book Project: Thank you for helping me realize my dream of distributing at least one copy of each of my books to every jail and prison supported by the Prison Book Project (close to three thousand and counting!). None of this work could have been accomplished without you and the wonderful volunteers at your organization.

To Jack and Scottie Barnes of Forgiven Ministry, their staff, and volunteers: It was an honor and a privilege to serve alongside you at "One Day with God." I was forever changed by my experience at the North Carolina Correctional Institution for Women in Raleigh. Thank you for your many years of faithful service and for answering God's call.

To those who have financially sown into The Vivian Foundation: God reminds us in his Word that he loves a cheerful giver. Thank you to our many donors for your faithful giving and support. The Kunes Family Foundation deserves special mention for their generous and timely provisions that allowed us to reach countless lives behind bars. We would not be where we are today without your family's generosity. Gregg, I am eternally grateful that you answered God's call and prayerfully considered and acted upon each blessing he asked you to bestow. Thank you for being a special blessing in my life.

And to Jesus Christ, the love of my life: What a journey this has been! This is our story, and to God be the glory.

Receive it! Speak it! Believe it!

Endnotes

1 Charles Stanley, "The Truth about the Trinity," Daily Devotions, News and Information, posted on February 21, 2017, https://808bo.com/2017/02/21/charles-stanley-the-truth-about-the-trinity/.

2 Stanley, "The Truth about the Trinity."

3 Brian and Candice Simmons, *Not Guilty: Be Free to Experience God's Love* (Savage, MN: Broadstreet Publishing, 2023), 12.

4 Tim Tebow, "The John 3:16 Story," Lifeway Voices, January 31, 2019, voices.lifeway.com.

5 Ruth Ann Nylen, *The Radical Power of God* (Land O' Lakes, FL: Mobilize Press, 2011), 65.

6 Robert Heidler, *Experiencing the Spirit: Developing a Living Relationship with the Holy Spirit* (Ventura, CA: Renew Books, 1998), 48.

7 Robert Heidler, *Experiencing the Spirit*, 48.

8 *NLT Parallel Study Bible* (Carol Stream, IL: Tyndale House Publishers, 2011), 2028.

9 Sarah Young, *Jesus Calling: Enjoying Peace in His Presence* (Nashville, TN: Thomas Nelson, 2004), 48.

10 A. J. Russell, *God Calling* (Uhrichsville, OH: Barbour Publishing, 1989), 64–65.

11 Eileen Egan, *Suffering into Joy: What Mother Teresa Teaches about True Joy* (Ann Arbor, MI: Servant Publications, 1994).

12 *NLT Chronological Life Application Study Bible* (Carol Stream, IL: Tyndale House Publishers, 2015).

13 Joyce Meyer, *Managing Your Emotions: Instead of Your Emotions Managing You* (Tulsa, OK: Harrison House, Inc., 1997), 168.

14 "Children and Families of the Incarcerated Fact Sheet," Rutgers University, accessed May 28, 2015, https://nrccfi.camden.rutgers.edu/files/nrccfi-fact-sheet-2014.pdf.

15 Charles Stanley, *The Source of My Strength: Relying on the Life-Changing Power of Jesus Christ to Heal Our Wounded Hearts* (Nashville, TN: Thomas Nelson, 2005), 135.

16 Max Lucado, *A Love Worth Giving: Living in the Overflow of God's Love* (Nashville, TN: W Publishing Group, 2006), 53.

17 Lucado, *A Love Worth Giving*, 54.

18 Rick Warren, *God's Power to Change Your Life* (Grand Rapids, MI: Zondervan, 2006), 203.

19 Warren, *God's Power to Change Your Life*, 213.

20 "Death Row," Death Penalty Information Center, accessed December 15, 2021, https://deathpenaltyinfo.org/death-row/overview.

21 "Types of Empathy," Skills You Need, accessed April 22, 2020, https://www.skillsyouneed.com/ips/empathy-types.html.

22 Wendy Sawyer and Peter Wagner, "Mass Incarceration: The Whole Pie 2020," Prison Policy Initiative, March 24, 2020, https://www.prisonpolicy.org/reports/pie2020.html.

About the Author

K atie Scheller was born and raised in Racine, Wisconsin. After she fell from the corporate ladder and hit rock bottom, God closed the door on her career and lovingly opened the door of a jail cell. After her time in prison, Katie felt led to establish The Vivian Foundation, a 501(c)(3) nonprofit organization dedicated to helping inmates and children of incarcerated parents.

Katie's first book, *Call Me Vivian*, was published in 2016 and exposed the truth behind her struggle with sexual sin, the battle for her heart, and the transforming power of God's love. Through Katie's heartache, pain, and countless years of searching, readers gain a deeper understanding of God's wonderful gifts of grace and forgiveness.

Vivian's Call, Katie's second book and sequel to *Call Me Vivian*, continues the true story of her life as former inmate 09902089 during her two-year stay in prison and beyond. Witness how God orchestrated events throughout Katie's life and how she answered her calling.

Step into Prison, Step Out in Faith builds upon Katie's life experiences before, during, and after her incarceration. It includes excerpts from her first two books as well as insightful, expanded biblical teachings. The book demonstrates that God truly works everything for good and encourages readers to never give up regardless of where they find themselves in life.

When Katie is not writing or managing The Vivian Foundation, she enjoys spending her summers with her family in Wisconsin and her winters with her friends in Florida. She has three children, Mike, Jenny, and Brian, and six grandchildren: Nicholas, Benjamin, Colin, Landon, Tyler, and McKenzie.

About The Vivian Foundation

T he American criminal justice system holds almost two million people in 1,566 state prisons, 102 federal prisons, 1,510 juvenile correctional facilities, and 2,850 local jails.[22] In the United States, 2.7 million children have a mother or father behind bars, and approximately 10 million children have experienced parental incarceration at some point in their lives.

Established in 2015, The Vivian Foundation is a 501(c)(3) nonprofit charitable organization dedicated to helping inmates and their children. The mission of the foundation is to raise money and provide Christian resources to prison ministries and other nonprofits supporting families impacted by incarceration.

Katie Scheller

The Vivian Foundation has donated hundreds of thousands of Christian resources to ministries across the United States. Today, the organization's primary focus is providing books, Bibles, and devotionals to incarcerated men and women and their children.

We stand on God's promise in Isaiah 55:11: "It is the same with my word. I send it out, and it always produces fruit." Every dollar sown into The Vivian Foundation comes with a heavenly guarantee to bear fruit.

Will you prayerfully consider sharing God's love and supporting our mission to help these families? Please visit our website at thevivianfoundation.com. Tax deductible donations can also be mailed to: The Vivian Foundation, P.O. Box 44601, Racine, Wisconsin 53404–7012.